TOBIAS SMOLLETT

by Robert Giddings

GREENWICH EXCHANGE
LONDON

Other books by Robert Giddings:

The Tradition of Smollett, (1967)

You Should see me in Pyjamas, (1981)

The Changing World of Dickens, (1983)

J.R.R. Tolkien: This Far Land, (1986)

Musical Quotes and Anecdotes, (1984)

True Characters (with Alan Bold), (1984)

The Book of Rotters (with Alan Bold), (1985)

Mark Twain: a Sumptuous Variety, (1985)

Matthew Arnold: between Two Worlds, (1986)

Who was really Who in Fiction (with Alan Bold), (1987)

The War Poets (1914 - 1918), (1988)

Screening the Novel (with Keith Selby and Chris Wensley), (1989)

Literature and Imperialism, (1991)

Echoes of War, (1991)

The Author the Book and the Reader, (1991)

Imperial Echoes, (1995)

GREENWICH EXCHANGE

First published in Great Britain in 1995

Tobias Smollett
by Robert Giddings © Copyright 1995

Printed and Bound by Priory Press Ltd, Holywood, N. Ireland

ISBN 1-871551-21-8

CONTENTS

Chronology   vi

I   Biography of a Writer   1

II   Works: Smollett and the Novel: 27
         The Adventures of Roderick Random;
         The Adventures of Peregrine Pickle

III   Works: *The Adventures of Ferdinand Count Fathom;*   44
         The Life and Adventures of Sir Launcelot Greaves

IV   Works: *The Expedition of Humprey Clinker*   47

V   Critical Overview: Smollett Today   58

Select Bibliography   74

SMOLLETT: CHRONOLOGY

1721   Tobias George Smollett born at Dalquhurn, Dumbartonshire, baptised at the parish church of Cardross, Dumbartonshire, on 19 March. He was the son of Archibald Smollett, youngest son of Sir James Smollett, Laird of Bonhill, a devout Whig, supporter of he Act of Union 1707.

1735   After attending Dumbarton Grammar School and Glasgow University, Smollett works at an apothecary's in Glasgow
William Hogarth, *The Rake's Progress*
Rene Lesage, *Gil Blas*

1736   Apprenticed to William Stirling and John Gordon, surgeons in Glasgow on 30 May.

1738   "Jenkins Ear" debate in Parliament. (Walpole delays declaration of war with Spain until October 1739)
Britain sends reinforcements to the Mediterranean. Ships and troops sent to Georgia and West Indies
Samuel Johnson, *London, A Poem*

1739   Goes to London, hoping to get his play, *The Regicide*, staged. He fails. On 4 December he successfully takes the Examination at Barber Surgeons' Hall, London.
Awarded warrant as Surgeon's Second Mate on 3 April, and sails with HMS *Chichester* to Jamaica, on Cartegena (Columbia) Expedition (26 October — January 1741)

1740   Samuel Richardson, *Pamela*

1741   Failure of Cartegena expedition. Of 8,000 troops landed, only 3,500 survive.
War of Jenkins Ear ends
Smollett returns to England (September)

1742   Henry Fielding , *Joseph Andrews*

1743   William Hogarth, *Marriage a la Mode*
Alexander Pope, *The Dunciad* (last edition in the poet's

lifetime)

Marries Anne Lascelles, daughter of a Jamaica planter, and attempts to establish himself as a surgeon, with premises in Downing Street, and later in Mayfair and Curzon Street.

1744   Henry Fielding, *Jonathan Wild the Great.*
Death of Alexander Pope

1745   Death of Robert Walpole
Charles Edward Stewart, the Young Pretender, lands in Eriskay 25 July. By September the Jacobites take Edinburgh and defeat an English army at Prestonpans on 21 September

1746   Charles Edward Stewart victorious at Falkirk, but routed at Culloden 16 April. Followed by suppression of Clan organisation. The Young Pretender escapes to France with Flora MacDonald's help.
Handel's *Judas Maccabeus*, oratorio (to celebrate Cumberland's victory at Culloden)
Smollett writes *The Tears of Scotland.*
Smollett writes opera libretto for John Rich, *Alceste* (never produced).
Publishes *Advice*, "a dialogue between Poet and Friend".

1747   George Lyttleton, 1st Baron Lyttleton, *Monody*
Answers Lyttleton's *Monody* with *Burlesque Ode*
Publishes *Reproof* (verse satire) and works on translation of Rene Lesage's *Gil Blas*

1748   Peace of Aix-la-Chapelle ends War of the Austrian Succession Travel to Europe again possible.
Samuel Richardson, *Clarissa.*
Smollett's daughter, Elizabeth, born.
Publishes *Roderick Random* (January)
In October, Smollett publishes his translation of Lesage's *Gil Blas.*

1749   Publishes his drama, *The Regicide* (June).
In the Autumn he tours Flanders, Holland and parts of France, visits Paris
Henry Fielding, *Tom Jones*
Samuel Johnson, *Irene* and *The Vanity of Human Wishes*

1750	Smollett obtains degree of M.D. from Mariscal College, Aberdeen. Visits Paris and the Low Countries Samuel Johnson starts The Rambler
1751	David Hume, Enquiry Concerning the Principles of Morals. Publishes *Peregrine Pickle* in February, a *success de scandale* as a result of its attacks on Lyttleton, Fielding, Cibber and Lady Vane.
1752	Henry Fielding, *Amelia* Attempts to establish himself as a physician in Bath, by residing there during the season (- 1755) In January Smollett publishes *Habbakkuk Hilding*, a satiric attack on fellow Novelist, Henry Fielding. In March Smollett publishes *An Essay on the External Use of Water, With Particular Remarks Upon the Present Method of Using the Mineral Waters at Bath, in Somersetshire.*
1753	Samuel Richardson, *Sir Charles Grandison* In February Smollett publishes *Ferdinand Count Fathom* Settles in Monmouth House, Lawrence Street, Chelsea and works as editor, journalist, compiler. Visits Scotland for the first time for for fifteen years (between June and November)
1754	Henry Fielding dies. Edits and publishes Alexander Drummond's Travels *Through Germany, Italy, Greece and Parts of Asia* Publishes *Histories of Germany, France and Italy.*
1755	Lisbon earthquake, 30,000 killed Samuel Johnson, *Dictionary of the English Language* Henry Fielding, *Journal of a Voyage to Lisbon* (posthumous) Publishes his translation of Cervantes' *Don Quixote* *Roderick Random* published in its fourth edition. Begins work on *A Complete History of England* (published 1757-1758)
1756	Britain declares war on France (Seven Years War)

Publishes *An Account of the Expedition Against Carthegena and A Compendium of Authentic and Entertaining Voyages.* Founds *The Critical Review*, (until 1763)

1757 Publishes *History of England*
January to May, Smollett's farce, *The Reprisal*, staged at Theatre Royal, Drury Lane, (published 1757 in May)

1758 Samuel Johnson, *The Idler* (-1760)
In March publishes the second, revised edition, of *Peregrine Pickle.*
In May publishes savage attack on Admiral Sir Charles Knowles, surveyor and engineer at the Cartegena Expedition, and Governor of Jamaica 1752-56, in *The Critical Review.*

1759 Samuel Johnson, *Rasselas*
Publishes *Universal History*

1760 Death of George II, succeeded by George III
Laurence Sterne, *Tristram Shandy*, volumes I and II
Begins the *British Magazine* (January issue begins serialisation of *The Adventures of Sir Launcelot Greaves*, until December 1761)
From November to February 1761 Smollett imprisoned in King's Bench for libel of Admiral Knowles
Begins work on the Continuation of *The Complete History of England.*

1761 Begins publication of *Works of Voltaire* (- 1774)

1762 Lord Bute becomes First Lord of the Treasury
John Wilkes edits *The North Briton* (- 1763)
Samuel Johnson granted Civil List pension of £300 a year
Edits *The Briton* from 29 May to the 12 February 1763 (which supports the government of Lord Bute)
Health begins to deteriorate, he tries to find employment abroad in warmer climate.

1763 Peace of Paris ends Seven Years War
Bute's ministry falls, succeeded by George Grenville
John Wilkes attacks King's Speech in Number 45 of *The North Briton*

James Boswell meets Samuel Johnson
Publishes Continuation of *The History of England*
Elizabeth, Smollett's daughter, aged fifteen, dies on 3 April.
Health begins seriously to decline.
Travels with wife and friends to the continent with friends.
Between November 1763 and April 1765 he resides at Nice.

1765 Horace Walpole, *The Castle of Otranto*
Samuel Johnson, *Works of William Shakespeare*
In July returns to England.

1766 Oliver Goldsmith, *The Vicar of Wakefield*
Publishes *Travels Through France and Italy*, and visits Bath
and Scotland (May to August)
Laurence Sterne, *Tristram Shandy* completed.

1768 Laurence Sterne, *A Sentimental Journey*
Publishes *The Present State of All Nations* (begun 1760)
Leaves England for Italy, settles near Leghorn (Livorno)

1769 The *Letters of Junius* attack George III and ministers.
In April publishes vicious political satire, *The Adventures of an Atom*

1771 Publishes *Humphry Clinker* (June)
Dies at Leghorn, on 17 September, aged fifty one.

1773 Smollett's *Ode to Independence*, (written in 1766) published
posthumously

1776 Smollett's translation of *Fenelon's Adventures of Telemachus*
published posthumously

I BIOGRAPHY OF A WRITER

Mr Smollett, aged 50 years; man of historical talent: asthmatic, suffering from chronic colic, diarrhoea, convulsions, fever. Has vigour; passionate and fiery temperament....He died from asthma and consumption....in the night of September 17..... A man of developed talents, suffering from the outrages of human life, almost a misanthrope. He lived eighteen years with his wife in perfect harmony, and by whom he had a daughter, who wrote poetry. Was of a very choleric disposition, but reflective, and devoted to political and historical study.

Note by Smollett's physician, Signor Pera, who treated him during his last illness, September 1771.

Britain in the Early 18th Century

Tobias George Smollett was born in 1721 and died in 1771. He was born at a time when Britain was recovering from political and economic instabilities. During his early life Britain experienced the political and economic stability of the Whig oligarchy (mainly the achievement of Sir Robert Walpole), survived a major rebellion and saw the Protestant Succession consolidated in the House of Hanover. During his adulthood Britain triumphed in a series of European and colonial wars and became established as a leading European and imperial nation — dominating trade with North America, the West Indies and India.

The Union between England and Scotland, under the name of Great Britain, provided for one parliament to which Scotland returned Members, and the adoption of one flag. This political stability was threatened by Jacobite rebellions in 1715 and 1745, led by descendants of James II, but these were successfully quashed, and the Jacobite threat finally laid to rest at the the battle of Culloden 1746. The War of the Spanish Succession was concluded by the Treaty of Utrecht in 1713, in which Britain gained territory in North America, and Gibraltar and Minorca were ceded to Britain. These were signs of Britain's growing mercantile and imperial importance. The wave of speculation which collapsed in January 1720, in a financial crisis known as the "South Sea Bubble", brought Robert Walpole to the forefront of British politics, a position he was to occupy until nearly the middle of the century. Walpole, leader of the Whig party, prime minister in all but name, ensured Britain's steady economic expansion by protecting and encouraging the nation's overseas trade and keeping Britain out of foreign wars.

The Smollett Family: his Early Life

Smollett, the novelist, was born in Dalquhurn, Dumbartonshire. His father, Archibald, was the youngest son of Sir James Smollett, laird of Bonhill, a zealous Whig who had been knighted by William III. Tobias was baptised at Cardross on 19 March 1721. Archibald Smollett died when the boy was only two years old but Sir James allowed the widowed mother to live at Dalquhurn with her three children. The boy did well at the Grammar School in Dumbarton, showing an aptitude for the classics. While he was at school he read George Buchanan's *Rerum Scoticarum Historia*, (one of the main sources of Scottish history) which contained an account of the murder of James I of Scotland at Perth in 1437, which Smollett was to use as the basis of his first major literary endeavour — the ill-fated tragedy *The Regicide*. John Moore, the celebrated physician, who knew Smollett at school and was his earliest biographer, testified to Smollett's learning and creative abilities. Smollett had a deep love of Scotland, and his strong identification with the land of his birth persisted throughtout his life.

After Sir James Smollett's death in 1731 Tobias's mother no longer benefited from his allowance. She was compelled to leave Dalquhurn, moving to Edinburgh, where she took an apartment in St John Street. Meanwhile, in 1736 Tobias was sent to Glasgow University to study Latin, Greek and Mathematics. It was resolved that he should study to become a doctor, and consequently he changed to courses in surgery and medicine.

His cousin, James of Bonhill, arranged for him to become an

apprentice to John Gordon, a Glasgow doctor and apothecary who later became a well known consulting surgeon. Smollett remained here until 1739, when he decided to try his fortunes down south, partly for reasons of his health, as he suffered from a bad chest. Like the young Scottish hero of his first novel, *Roderick Random*, he travelled to London with few clothes, a case of instruments, a few guineas and a couple of books, including Richard Wiseman's *Surgery*, the standard textbook of the day. John Moore comments that he had little money but many introductions:

> Whether they, the family, designed to make up for the scantiness of the one by their profusion of the other is uncertain; but he has often been heard to declare, that their liberality in the last article was prodigious.

Smollett also took with him that which he clearly regarded as his passport to security, celebrity and good fortune - the manuscript of his tragedy, *The Regicide*.

Beginnings of Modern Commercial Publishing

Smollett arrived in London at a period of considerable development in printing, publishing and public literacy - a crucial period in the history of literary production and consumption. He was himself to play a significant part in these developments, and, professionally, to figure in a transitional role. He came to London, optimistically aspiring to literary fame with a drama. The theatre had for a couple of centuries been the traditional pathway to literary fame and fortune. Smollett, however, arrived at the metropolis in time professionally to participate in the foundation of modern publishing. The Copyright Act of 1710 gave authors' rights protection for fourteen years. Authorship and commercial publishing gained a considerable fillip from this Act. During his early childhood circulating libraries began to flourish in London and the larger provincial cities and resorts (such as Bath) where members, for a subscription, could borrow popular works of the day. Thomas Sendall established a very successful circulating library in Bristol in 1728. This system thrived throughout Smollett's working life.

Although the early 18th century is not noted as a period of great educational improvement, there is some evidence that basic literacy slowly increased. The Society for Promoting Christian Knowledge was founded at the close of the 17th century, and by 1723 had established 1,329 charity schools. Their sparse curriculum - reading and writing, scripture, and, for bright boys, arithmetic (needlework for the girls) did at least provide generation after generation of new readers, though, as M.G.Jones comments in his *Charity School Movement* (1938), the general aim might well have been to establish social discipline among the poor and "condition the children for their primary duty in life as hewers of wood and drawers of water". In Wales the support given by the people was very considerable. The SPCK was established in Ireland early in the century, but the educational state of the people was an indictment of the Anglo-Irish ascendancy. Scottish education was traditionally more advanced than elsewhere in the kingdom. Since John Knox the Scottish Church had been responsible for the elementary education of all children of whatever social class. This was especially noticeable in the Lowlands (the clan system and wide spread nature of the population made education problematic in the Highlands). The Scottish SPCK established technical schools in 1738. After Cullodon the policy of unifying Lowlands and Highlands was an incentive to educational development: indeed, much of the money derived from forfeited Highland feudal estates was spent on Scottish school development. Gaelic was excluded from schools and instruction was entirely in English. Dr Johnson commented in Journey to the Western Islands of Scotland 1773:

> ...there was perhaps never any change of national manners so quick, so great and so general, as that which has operated in the Highlands, by the last conquest and subsequent laws ... Schools are erected in which English only is taught....

These were the circumstances which would enable Smollett to

earn his living as a man of letters. Indeed, he is an outstanding early example of professional authorship. With little independent income no support from patrons, Smollett supported himself by his pen- with journalism, popular histories, collections of voyages and translations as well as novels.

Economics of 18th Century Authorship

It is worth considering the economics of authorship in Smollett's time. Dr Samuel Johnson (1709-1784) estimated that the cost of living averaged around £30 a year. Writers traditionally had been able to support themselves by receiving sums from wealthy patrons, who paid for the privilege of having works dedicated to them. Thomas Gordon (1691-1750), a jobbing author and translator of Tacitus and Sallust who worked for Sir Robert Walpole, summed up the patron/dedication nexus:

> I have known an author praise an Earl for twenty pages together, though he knew nothing of him but that he had money to spare. He made him wise, just and religious for no reason in the world but in hopes to find him charitable; and gave him a most bountiful heart because he himself had an empty stomach..

Joseph Addison, who celebrated Marlborough's victory at Blenheim in *The Campaign* and satirised the Tories in his journalism, was rewarded with government appointments and retired with a pension of £1,500 a year in 1718. Others who came out publicly for the Whigs — Steele, Congreve, and several leading scientists — thrived under them. Under James II Dryden had been rewarded for his support of the royalist High Tory cause with the Poet Laureateship and a pension of £300 a year. Pope was Tory in the period of Whig ascendancy, but the sales of his and others' translations of Homer (estimated as at least £13,000) made him independent of Whig magnates. His position partly secured, supported by his close friendship with the arch Tory Bolingbroke, Pope was in a position to attack Walpole and the Whig oligarchy in his *Moral Essays* and *Imitations of*

Horace. Swift satirized the Whigs during the Tory administration, and was made Dean of St Patrick's Cathedral in Dublin. His ecclesiastical career was subsequently blighted with the ascendancy of the Whigs after 1720.

The Laureateship was used mainly to reward writers' political loyalty. Dryden earned it for crowing up the Stewart cause, and lost it to his Whig rival, Thomas Shadwell, in 1688 (Shadwell had attacked him in *The Medal* as John Bayes). Laurence Eusden was given it in 1718 for his poem flattering the Duke of Newcastle and celebrating his marriage: the Duke was Lord Chamberlain and the Laureateship was in his gift. Colley Cibber became Laureate in 1730 as a reward for his long term support of the Hanoverian cause, particularly for his comedy *The Non Juror* (1717 a version of Moliere's *Tartuffe*) for which he received two hundred guineas from George I.

Smollett Seeks a Patron

Smollett was to have personal experience of the humiliating ritual of seeking patronage. He failed to get theatre managers interested in *The Regicide* (Charles Fleetwood and Willoughby Lacy at Drury Lane showed no interest; nor did James Quin or John Rich at Covent Garden). He then attempted to find a patron. He sent it to Lord Chesterfield. Chesterfield handed it over to William Garrick, who was in the Drury Lane management. In a letter dated September 1746 Garrick mentions that he has:

> .....a play , sent to me by my Lord Chesterfield, and wrote by our Smollett. It is a Scotch story, but it won't do, and yet recommended by his Lordship and patron-ised by Ladies of quality, what can I say or do? Must I believe my judgement, or run the risk of being thought impertinent and disobliging by the great folk?

Smollett went to see Garrick; but his drama (deservedly, it should be added) was not to be staged. Smollett never forgot this humiliating and insulting treatment. He satirised John Rich's popular successes in pantomime in his *Reproof* and he was to rehearse his experiences in

6

his first novel, *Roderick Random,* in which Garrick is caricatured as Mr Marmozet, Chesterfield as the supercilious Lord Sheerwit, and Lacy, Quin and Rich as Brayer, Bellower and Vandal. Smollett had great hopes of George Lyttleton, later Baron Lyttleton, who had patronised fellow Scots writers James Thompson and David Mallet. But Lyttleton didn't even bother to read *The Regicide.* Smollett never forgave him. When Lyttleton was widowed in 1747 and expressed his grief in his poem *Monody,* Smollett viciously satirised this in a *Burlesque Ode,* pretending to lament the death of his grandmother.

Ten years later, in June 1749, Smollett published *The Regicide,* together with a Preface, more brilliant and vigorous than the play itself, an attack on the what he calls the "prostitution" of authorship, the treatment he had and on the literary-patronage system itself:

Abuse of prerogative...
   prevails so much at present, and is so generally overlooked, that it is almost ridiculous to lament the situation of authors, who must either at once forgo all opportunities of acquiring reputation in dramatic poetry, or humble themselves, so as to sooth the pride, and humour the petulance of a mere Goth, who, by the most preposterous delegation of power, may become the arbiter of this kind of writing....

Decline of Patronage

But the system of seeking patronage and repaying favours with mellifluous dedications was soon to die out. It began to be replaced by a custom of genuine dedication of affection and admiration. Fielding dedicated his *Historical Register* 1737 to the public at large ("from the great to the multitude"). Samuel Johnson's career spanned the end of patronage and the beginnings of professional authorship in the modern sense. Although his celebrated quarrel with Lord Chesterfield is usually glibly referred to as the "end of literary patronage" it should be remembered that, in fact, Johnson himself did live from writing. He negotiated on a business footing with editors and publishers, from his arrival in London until he was granted a Civil List pension by George

III in 1762. At one stage he was employed as writer and editor on the *Gentleman's Magazine* for £100 a year. Nevertheless, his famous letter to Lord Chesterfield during the quarrel over the publication of Johnson's *Dictionary of the English Language* in 1755 is a significant moment in the history of professional authorship:

> .....Is not a patron, my Lord, one who looks with unconcern on a man struggling for his life in the water, and when he has reached ground, encumbers him with help?....

Johnson was well acquainted with the humiliation of patronage. In *The Vanity of Human Wishes* (1749), he had listed a scholar's ills as including "toil, envy, want, the patron and the jail". In his *Dictionary* he defines a patron as "commonly a wretch who supports with insolence, and is paid with flattery".

The first half of the 18th century was notorious for its political nepotism and "patronage". Governments were ever ready to bribe journalists and silence critics with bribes, rewards or threats. It has been estimated that between 1732 and 1742 Walpole spent £50,000 of Treasury funds in buying the support of the press. Paradoxically, it was massive control by means of a system of political jobbery and manipulation — possibly unequalled in British parliamentary history — which caused the decline of patronage. At last, Dr Johnson himself was able to declare: "We have done with patronage".

Authorship as a Career: Indolent Smollett, Trifling Johnson

By mid century, developments in printing, publishing, marketing and consumption of books had considerably reduced the importance of wealthy patronage from among the land-owning classes and aristocracy. Petulantly, they in turn affected a disdain for men of letters. Even one as enlightened and cultivated as Horace Walpole, himself a novelist, could comment on indolent Smollett, trifling Johnson, piddling Goldsmith.....how little have they contributed to the glory of a period in which all arts, all sciences are encouraged and rewarded.

During the 18th century, then, it was possible for a writer of enterprise and energy to sustain himself by his pen. Printing and publishing had originally been a single combined enterprise, monopolised in Britain by the Stationers' Company, which was granted its Royal Charter in 1557. Fear of religious controversy and political sedition had encouraged authorities to restrict publication by censorship in various forms — the Star Chamber (abolished by the Long Parliament in 1641), direct censorship, a Licensing Act which only allowed approved publishers to print and distribute material (this lapsed in 1695) and economic restrictions (such as the Stamp Act 1712).

Printing technology advanced throughout the period of Smollett's literary career.The developments in the industry were led by such pioneers as William Caslon (1692-1766) and his son, William Caslon (1720-1728), who who cut type for printers and popularised the "old face" type, still in use today. John Baskerville (1706-1775) developed new type face designs — his quarto edition of Virgil 1756 was the first of over fifty beautiful editions which eventually included Milton, Juvenal, Addison, Congreve, Horace, Catullus.

Author-Publisher Relationships

The seeds of the separation between author, publisher and printer had been present in embryo in the industry from its earliest days. The author seldom physically produced and distributed copies of his own work. He negotiated some kind of financial relationship with a businessman who might possibly print and distribute copies, or might pay another to print them, and then undertake to market them in volume form. The enterprise might be underwritten by a patron, or the publisher might provide all the venture capital himself. Sales produced the profit, and the writer received an agreed share called a "royalty". Christopher Barker (1529-1599), the Queen's Printer, who purchased the patent to print the Old and New Testament in English in 1577, and later for all state printing and religious works, wrote in the late 1550's that as booksellers began to make money, so they began to acquire authors' copyrights, and to become publishers themselves:

> The booksellers, being grown the greater and wealthier in number, have now many of the best copyrights and keep no printing house, neither bear any charge of letter (type) or other furniture, but only pay for the workmanship.... Some of them, though their skill be little or nothing in the execution of the art, have more judgement to govern and order matters of printing than some printers themselves. But unless some printers be well maintained, it will bring both the one and the other to confusion and extreme poverty.

Examination of title pages of books produced in the 16th and 17th century discloses evidence of the birth of a genuine publishing industry, separated from printing. The first pages of a book may say "Printed by" — some say "Printed by Such-and-Such for So-and-So" and others "Printed by Such-and-Such for So-and-So and Sold by etc" Here you may see the three trades working in co-operation — the printer, the publisher and the bookseller.

By the end of the 17th century the prototype of the modern publisher had emerged. In 1710 the first British Copyright Act had at last given writers the opportunity to negotiate some return for their creative labours. For a down payment (if they decided to sell their copyright outright) or an agreed proportion of their sales (royalties) they allowed a publisher to print and distribute their work. The publisher actually had nothing except his costs. The printer had the paper, the type-face and the ink and the bookseller had the books. The publisher's role in the literary industry was and is, that of the ultimate middle-man; but without him, there would be no industry.

This was the age which brought forth the founding fathers of British publishing — Jacob Tonson and his nephew, Barnaby Lintot, William Straham, William Taylor, Andrew Millar, Thomas Longman,

Robert Dodsley. It was the hard work as well as the greed and cunning of these men which gave the world the works of Defoe, Richardson, Fielding, Gay, Johnson, Goldsmith and Sterne. Writers of books were beginning to be professionally paid for their work. In 1742 Dodsley paid Edward Young £220 for *Night Thoughts* and Henry Fielding pocketed £183, 10 shillings and 10 pence for *Joseph Andrews.* Seven years later *Tom Jones* earned Fielding £700 and in 1752 *Amelia* brought him £1,000. Others, less widely known however, were thoroughly exploited.

It is interesting to draw some conclusions about the taste of the consumers at this time. Fiction, it seems, was not in great demand, and was very expensive. Readers tended to borrow new novels from the circulating libraries, which was a major diversion and source of conversation at the fashionable resorts, such as Bath. Collections of voyages, travels, natural history and popular histories were in greater demand. Books on medicine (much of it quackery) were lucrative. John Hill, who worked as an apothecary and quack doctor in James Street, Covent Garden, was alleged to have made an income of some £1,500 a year by various compilations on diagnosis, medicines and cures. There was an appetite for history. William Robertson published his *History of Scotland* in 1759 himself and earned £600, while his *Charles V* (1769) brought £4,500. Hume and Smollett wrote their *Histories* for Millar, who paid them £5,400 each. Lord Lyttleton was paid £3,000 for his *Life of Henry II* (1767-71) but Adam Smith was paid only £500 for his *Wealth of Nations.*

This was the world of professional authorship in which Smollett was to spend his working life. But, in the meantime, he was to experience in His Majesty's Royal Navy.

Smollett as Ship's Surgeon

On 4 December 1739 Smollett passed his examinations at Barber Surgeons' Hall. Realising that he was destined for disappointment so far as a career as the drama was concerned, he took advantage of the current pressing need for naval surgeons as a result of the war with Spain. He secured an appointment as a surgeon's mate on board HMS *Chichester*, which sailed on 26 October 1740 to reinforce the fleet of Admiral Edward Vernon in the West Indies. He was present at the catastrophically unsuccessful attack on Cartegena (Columbia) in 1741. He uses his experiences for the naval scenes in his novel, *Roderick Random* (1748). A further account appears in his *A Compendium of Voyages* (1756) The fleet returned to Jamaica, where he served as a surgeon to British troops. Here he met Anne Lascelles, a handsome Creole girl, daughter of a well-to-do planter, with an estate and slaves. It was agreed that they should marry when he returned to London, where he intended to set up as a surgeon in premises in Downing Street - and to, with characteristic obstinacy, continue attempts to launch his play, *The Regicide*. He married Anne (whom he called Nancy) in 1743, and lived a reasonably happy social life, keeping company with several of his fellow Scots in various coffee houses and taverns.

He was in such company on the evening of 23 April 1746 when the news reached London of the terrible and bloody defeat of Bonnie Prince Charlie and his rebels at Culloden. While the mobs in the city celebrated the victory, - dancing in the streets, fireworks blazing in the sky and bonfires flaming and smoking everywhere - Smollett sat in a tavern room and, while his friends sullenly played at cards, wrote his poem, *The Tears of Scotland*. Smollett is seldom recognised as a poet, and this poem is infrequently reprinted, but as it shows an unsuspected aspect of his creative life, part of it is reproduced here:

Mourn, hapless Caledonia, mourn
Thy banish'd peace, thy laurels torn!
Thy sons, for valour long renown'd,
Lie slaughter'd on their native ground;
Thy hospitable roofs no more
Invite the stranger to the door;
In smoky ruins sunk they lie,
The monuments of cruelty.
The wretched owner sees, afar,

His all become the prey of war;
Bethinks him of his babes and wife,
Then smites his breast, and curses life.

Smollett's medical practice did not flourish and so he moved to what was then by no means a fashionable an area, Curzon Street. With money the couple obtained from the estates in Jamaica they moved to Monmouth House, (now demolished) in 24, Lawrence Street, in south west London, which had been the home of the Duke of Monmouth's widow. Dr John Moore describes him at this time:

> The person of Smollett was stout and well proportioned, his countenance engaging, his manner reserved, with a certain air of dignity that seemed to indicate that he was not unconscious of his own powers. He was of a disposition so humane and generous, that he was ever ready to serve the unfortunate, and on some occasions to to assist them beyond what his circumstances could justify......
>
> Free from vanity, Smollett had a considerable share of pride, and great sensibility: his passions were easily moved, and too impetuous when roused: his could not conceal his contempt of folly, his detestation of fraud, nor refrain from proclaiming his indignation against every form of oppression.
>
> Though Smollett possessed a versatility of style in writing, which he could accommodate to every character, he had no suppleness in his conduct. His learning, diligence, and natural acuteness would have rendered him eminent in the science of medicine, had he persevered in that profession: other parts of his character were ill-suited for augmenting his practice. He could neither stoop to impose on credulity nor humour caprice.
>
> He was of an intrepid, independent, imprudent disposition, equally incapable of deceit and adulation, and more disposed to cultivate the acquaintance of those he could serve, than of those who could serve him. What a wonder that a man of his character was not, what is called, successful in life! (John Moore: Works of Tobias Smollett, With a Memoir 1797)

Smollett Begins his Professional Literary Career

Smollett now embarked on a period of considerable literary activity. His practice did not flourish and he decided to earn his living by his pen. He published two verse satires, *Advice* and *Reproof* (1746-

47) and was preparing a translation of the French novel *Gil Blas de Santillane* by Lesage, published in 1715 and 1724. This is a picaresque novel which tells the story of Gil Blas, son of humble parents who is packed off to go to University of Salamanca and meets many adventures on the way. He falls among thieves, becomes a quack doctor and is employed by the Archbishop of Granada, becomes secretary to the Prime Minister, falls from grace and finishes up in prison. His experiences chasten him and he retires to a quiet rural life. This tale of the vicissitudes of life is continually enlivened by brilliant characterisation and numerous comic episodes. It had a considerable influence on Smollett.

In January 1748 Smollett published his first novel, *The Adventures of Roderick Random*. The 1740's was a splendid decade for the English novel. In 1740 Samuel Richardson published *Pamela; or Virtue Rewarded*; Henry Fielding's parody of it, *Joseph Andrews*, followed in 1742. The next year Fielding published *Jonathan Wild the Great* and, in the same year which saw *Roderick Random*, Samuel Richardson published *Clarissa; or The History of a Young Lady*. Even with such competition this first novel by an obscure twenty seven-year old Scotsman was noticed.

Smollett embarked on this first major novel without prentice work behind him. *Roderick Random* is substantially autobiographical. It tells the story of a young Scot who, left penniless, seeks his fortune in the company of his old school friend, Strap. In London he fails to gain the patronage he needs for entry to the Royal Navy, but is eventually grabbed by the press-gang and serves in the Spanish war in the West Indies. He returns to London and falls in love with a young heiress, Narcissa, but is kidnapped by smugglers and taken to France, where he joins the army and fights in the battle of Dettingen, Bavaria. He now sets out to marry a lady of fortune. After many intrigues he loses all his money at cards. He now embarks on a career as a ship's surgeon. In his travels he meets his father, Don Roderigo, a wealthy trader. He marries Narcissa and Strap marries her maid, Williams.

The novel reached a wide readership. The young writer Catherine

Talbot, niece of Charles Talbot, the lord Chancellor, wrote enthusiastically in a letter that it was a strange and "low" book, but that she believed it very just:

......though not without some characters in it, and I believe some very just, though very wretched descriptions. Among others, there is the history of a poor tragedy author, ill used by actors and managers, that I think one cannot but be touched with, when one considers how many such kinds of scenes there are every day in real life. That wicked good-nature of the rich and great, that can see, and acknowledge merit in distress, speak it fair, promise high, raise expectations, and yet continue indolent, and do nothing to relieve it, is shewn in a striking manner; and so is the cruelty of delaying people, and putting them off from day to day, and many other inhumanities unfelt by the doers...

It was very successful, for a first novel. The two volumes were sold for sixteen shillings. Some figures survive in a ledger kept by the printer, William Strahan. Two thousand copies were issued. Between January 1748 and November 1749 a further six thousand five hundred copies were printed. The second edition appeared in April 1748 and a third followed in January 1750. A fourth edition was issued in August 1754. In the year before Smollett died, his first novel had reached its eighth edition in London. In one stride, he became a professional writer.

Smollett described the toils of authorship in *Roderick Random*, where he gave a satirical account of the patronage system, and again in *Peregrine Pickle* in which he gave an account of the emerging, modern publishing industry. He seemed to have, for the time being, sufficient work to pay his way in the world. The Peace of Aix-la-Chapelle, October 1748, opened France and the continent to travellers once more. In September 1749 Smollett toured Flanders, Holland and France (experiences he was to exploit in his next novel). The following year he was in the Low Countries, and after which he visited Paris. In February 1751 he published *The Adventures of Peregrine Pickle*. Henry Fielding's masterpiece, *Tom Jones*, had appeared in 1749, but even so the readership was not quite prepared for what Smollett had in store for them.

Once again, Smollett tells the story of a picaresque hero. His adventures take him to the continent. There are fine set piece scenes in Paris (Peregrine fights a duel with a musketeer and is imprisoned in the Bastille) and the Netherlands, as well as some incisive satire of social life and medical quackery in Bath. Peregrine attempts to earn a living as a magician and to enter parliament, is committed to the Fleet prison for debt - but eventually inherits his father's wealth and marries his lady love. The novel is remarkable for its rumbustious comicality and string of striking, original and memorable characters. As well as the clearly delineated portraits of Peregrine's parents, there is his loyal friend, Tom Pipes, and the old sea dog, Commodore Hawser Trunnion, who talks the special language of the old salt and lives in a garrison run with military precision, with his companion, the one-legged Lieutenant Hatchway. (There are echoes of these episodes in Uncle Toby and Corporal Trim in Sterne's *Tristram Shandy*, of Captain Cuttle in *Dombey and Son* and the Aged Parent in *Great Expectations*).

Peregrine Pickle gave the public much to talk about. There were recognisable, and usually satirical portraits of contemporaries — Fielding, Lyttleton, Colley Cibber — as well as the interpolation of the Memoirs of a Lady of Quality, which was notoriously the story of Frances Anne Hawes (1713-1788). She was a dowerless but very handsome young woman when she married Lord William Douglas in 1732, who died two years later. She then married William, second Viscount Vane and became notorious for profligacy and gambling. She was nicknamed "Lady Fanny". Horace Walpole commented in a letter of 13 March 1751:

..... My Lady Vane has literally published the Memoirs of her own life, only suppressing part of her lovers, no part of the success of the others with her: a degree of profligacy not to be accounted for; she does not want money, none of her stallions will raise her credit; and the number, all she had to brag of concealed!

Lady Mary Wortley Montagu, another great gossip of the time, commented:

> .... Her story rightly considered, would be more instructive to young women than any sermon I know. They may see there what mortification and variety of misery are the unavoidable consequences of gallantries. I think there is no rational creature that would not prefer the life of the strictest Carmelite to the round of hurry and misfortune she has gone through.....

Fame, but no Fortune.

Despite the fame this novel brought him, the financial returns were not commensurate. An experienced author had difficulty in gaining a good return on good sales. Not a great deal is known about the actual publishing history of his major works. Although the practice of using a single publisher was becoming more prevalent, Smollett seems to have used several. *Roderick Random* was published in 1748 by John Osborn of Paternoster Row. *Peregrine Pickle* was published in 1751 by R.Baldwin and J.Richardson of Paternoster Row, and D.Wilson and T.Durham of The Strand. His third novel, *Ferdinand Count Fathom*, was published in 1753 by William Johnston. Smollett's translation of *Don Quixote* appeared in 1755, published by T.Osborn, Thomas Longman and his nephew Thomas Longman, Andrew Miller, C.Hitch, L.Hawes, J.Hodges and J and J. Rivington. His next novel, *Sir Launcelot Greaves*, was serialised in his own *British Magazine* between January and December 1760. His *Travels Through France and Italy* appeared in 1766 published by R.Baldwin. *Humphry Clinker,* appeared in 1771, published by W.Johnston of Ludgate Street and B.Collins of Salisbury.

Our own perception of 18th century literary production is certainly different from that of Smollett and his contemporaries. Because of the nature of cultural production, consumption and the slow development of "classical" status, we tend to admire what we now recognise as the masterpieces of the 18th century — its poetry, classic stage comedies, novels, satires — and to forget that there was a vast contemporary appetite for travel books, collections of voyages, biographies, popular and sensational fiction, fashionable stage plays, popular histories and other ephemeral publications and hackwork material which has hardly survived and is of only historical interest now. As well as producing his "classic" fiction, Smollett toiled successfully for this market all his working life.

Pickle was a sensation, but the novelist, his wife and daughter could not survive long on the money brought in. This may be gleaned from a letter dated 11 February 1752, just after the successful publication of *Peregrine Pickle*, in which he records difficulties resulting from non-arrival of funds due from his wife's family in the West Indies and his consequent need to borrow substantial sums. Nevertheless his hospitality — especially to fellow authors — was celebrated. Many Scots who visited London called to enjoy his hospitality at Chelsea, including the notorious Peter Gordon, who abused his generosity severely (Gordon was a swindler whom Smollett eventually physically, thrashed). He returned to medical practice at Bath and contributed to the controversy then thriving between medical experts as to the best methods of using the waters. In March 1752 he published *An Essay on the External Use of Water, With Particular Remarks Upon the Present Method of Using the Mineral Waters at Bath, in Somersetshire, and A Plan for Rendering them more Safe, Agreeable and Efficacious*. It did not drum up trade; but it contains brilliant and detailed accounts of spa treatment invaluable to the medical historian and was reprinted in the 1935 bulletin of the Institute of Medicine. Smollett's experiences in Bath at this time are well used in his fiction, which contains memorably satiric accounts of medical practitioners of the day.

But he did not thrive. We find him earning £100 from George Drummond, Lord Provost of Edinburgh, for editing and revising his brother Alexander Drummond's *Travels Through Germany, Italy and Greece*. His novel *Ferdinand Count Fathom* was published in February 1753; but a letter of 27 May 1753 suggests that Smollett was still hard up. He was owed £1,000 from Jamaica by now. By November that year he writes "Never was I so much harassed with duns as now; a persecution which I owe to the detention of that remittance from Jamaica, which I have expected every day since last Christmas...." In August 1754 the fourth edition of *Random* appeared. February the following year saw the publication, supported by subscription, of his translation of *Don Quixote*. He had been working on this for about six years. Lady Mary Wortley Montagu, (a renowned wit and one of the greatest English letter writers) lamented the fact that a writer of Smollett's gifts should give over such time to translation. She wrote in a letter dated 1 January 1755 to her daughter: "I am sorry my friend Smollett loses his time in translations, he has certainly far more invention...." But Smollett's English translation of this classic was only the fourth to appear, and, allowing for the conventions of its time and place, it remains probably the best.

Since 1755 he had been engaged on *A Complete History of England from the Descent of Julius Caesar to the Treaty of Aix-la-Chapelle 1748, containing the Transactions of one Thousand Eight Hundred and Three Years*. This work, which was composed at the rate of a century a month began to appear in 1757, was written at a time when he continued to be pressed for money. A letter of 6 April 1756 records his state of affairs as well as interesting evidence about author-publisher agreements of the day:

> I have been last week threatened with writs of arrest; and some tradesmen in Chelsea have been so clamourous, that I actually promised to pay them in the beginning of this week. I had recourse to Mr Rivington [his publisher] who happens to be out of cash, in consequence of breaking up partnership with his brother. My proposal was, that he should advance £100 which would pay at the rate of four guineas per week, deducted from the History... He had no sort of objection to the scheme; and agrees to to join with me in security for the money, if it can be borrowed for six months or longer.

Smollett's optimism about this work was justified. The first edition of his *History of England* sold out and a second edition was published in weekly parts between 1758-1760 (and sold on average 10,000 copies). Smollett earned £2,000 and the publisher, Archibald Hamilton, made a fortune. The success of the *History* brought him other, similar, work, such as *Universal History*, in forty-four volumes which came out between 1759-1766.

Smollett as Journalist

At this stage of his career, Smollett became more seriously involved in journalism. In 1755 he visited Scotland for the first time since he had left his homeland. When he returned to Chelsea he was invited to join the editorial staff of a new High Tory, High Church literary magazine, planned to run in opposition to *Monthly Review* (a Whig journal founded in 1749 by Ralph Griffiths). Smollett's journal was *The Critical Review, or, Annals of Literature.* All the evidence suggests that though Smollett might not have been the editor of this journal in the modern sense, he was in virtual control of it. The opening Editorial certainly sounds like Smollett

> The candour and indulgence of the Public, will, we hope, excuse any little defects that may appear in the disposition of the articles that compose this first Essay; as we do not pretend to be altogether perfect as yet, in the mechanical part of our undertaking; and have been more studious to cater variety for our guests, than to arrange the dishes of the entertainment. ....

It can safely be concluded that one of his editorial colleagues was Archibald Hamilton, a fellow Scot from Edinburgh, who had been compelled to leave his native city for taking part in the Porteus Riots of 1736, and is a known close associate. Hamilton was a foreman in William Strahan's printing works. The early issues of *The Critical Review* were printed by R.Baldwin, at the Rose in Paternoster Row, but later editions were "Printed for A.Hamilton, Chancery Lane". This journal is now of considerable cultural and historical interest. It undertook to review a very wide range of contemporary publications, and, additionally, included much cultural and social comment. It may be seen as an early prototype of journalism we now take for granted - such as *The Spectator, New Statesman-Society, London Review of Books* etc.

In May 1758 Smollett published an article in the *Monthly Review* which severely took to task the reputation of Vice Admiral Sir Charles Knowles, who had served as Engineer and Surveyor during the expedition against Cartegena. (Smollett served on HMS *Chichester* during this engagement). Knowles entered a prosecution against Archibald Hamilton, as printer. Smollett found it most expedient to admit authorship, and he was fined £100 and committed to the King's Bench Prison for three months (November to February 1760-61). Here he was visited by Oliver Goldsmith, David Garrick and John Wilkes - evidence of the status he had by now achieved. He had of course long made up his quarrel with Garrick.

Smollett's literary labours during the 1760's were considerable. He worked on a continuation of his *History of England* and edited a compilation, *The Present State of All Nations*, in eight volumes (1764). He was also responsible for a small part of the translation of *The Works of M. de Voltaire: Translated from the French. With notes historical and critical* — the first of whose thirty-nine volumes appeared in 1761, the last in 1769. He was offered the post of editor of a new periodical, the *British Magazine, or, Monthly Repository for Gentlemen and Ladies*. The first issue appeared in January 1760, and it ran to December 1867. The first issues contained Smollett's latest novel, *Sir Launcelot Greaves*, in serial parts. It was the first English novel to appear in serial parts. It is thought by some to be his weakest novel, although the basic idea could have been developed into a brilliant satire. Others think it a neglected masterpiece. Smollett takes the idea of a modern, British, Don Quixote. He sallies forth in armour "to combat vice in all her forms, redress injuries, chastise oppression, protect the helpless and forlorn, relieve the indigent". There was much in Hanoverian Britain that such a deranged knight-errant could satirically expose. We are given interesting portraits of an election, the provincial magistracy, the King's Bench Prison and a lunatic asylum — but the performance whatever its merits, is certainly marred in places by the author's evident fatigue.

Smollett landed himself again in political controversy. In October

1761 Lord Bute, a fellow Scot, and an unpopular prime minister, sought his aid in whipping up some public support for his policies. He resolved to finance a journal, the *Briton,* and offered Smollett the editorship, which he accepted. When the first issue appeared on 29 May 1762, John Wilkes, the radical politician, although an opponent of the government's, paid Smollett a compliment. On hearing of Smollett's undertaking this journal he said: "It would seem that Bute, after the distributing all the places under government to his adherents, is determined to monopolise the wit also". But Smollett's paper was snuffed out by Wilkes' more incisive rejoinder, the *North Briton.* The controversy over Wilkes' attack on the King's Speech in Parliament in 1763 resulted in Wilkes' celebrated prosecution (and eventually secured considerable political freedom for the press including the right to report parliamentary proceedings). But in the raucous controversy, Smollett's magazine was overwhelmed by the popular clamour of Wilkes' *North Briton.* Its last issue was dated 12th February 1763.

Smollett's health now began to show serious signs of deterioration: he suffered a permanent cough, low fever and rheumatic pains. He hoped at one stage to find employment in a warmer climate. Then on, 3 April, that year his darling daughter, Elizabeth, died of consumption at the age of fifteen. He was distracted with grief. In a letter he wrote:

> Many a time did I stop my task and betake me to a game of romps with Betty, while my wife looked on smiling, and longing in her heart to join the sport; then back to the cursed round of duty.

In June that year he left London with his wife and lived in Nice between November 1763 to April 1765. He saw many sights, visiting Boulogne, Paris, Lyons, Montpellier, Rome, Genoa, Florence, Pisa, Aix en Provence, Toulon and Marseilles. There is a Rue Smollett in Nice to this day, but, as he wrote, he was very glad to return to Britain in July 1765:

> I am at last in a situation to indulge my view with a sight of Britain, after an

absence of two years; and indeed, you cannot imagine what pleasure I feel while I survey the White Cliffs of Dover.... Not that I am at all affected by the 'nescia qua dulcedine natalis soli' of Horace..... I am attached to my country, beause it is the land of liberty, cleanliness and convenience: but I love it still more tenderly, as the scene of all my interesting connections; as the habitation of my friends, for whose conversation, correspondence, and esteem, I wish alone to live.

In May 1766 the literary results of these travels was published as *Travels Through France and Italy*. The impressions of places and the opinions expressed are irascible, irritable and eccentric but they are wholly honest: totally Smollettian! Long past their use as travel writing, these pages are still valued as among the most brilliant and characteristic prose Smollett composed. His wayward and disenchanted views earned him Sterne's caricature of him as "Smelfungus" in *A Sentimental Journey* 1768:

I pity the man who can travel from Dan to Beersheba, and cry 'Tis all barren' — and so it is; and so is all the world to him who will not cultivate the fruit it offers. I declare, said I, clapping my hands cheerily together, that was I in a desert, I would find out wherewith in it to call forth my affection.... The learned SMELFUNGUS travelled from Boulogne to Paris — from Paris to Rome — and so on - but he set out with the spleen and the jaundice, and every object he passed by was discoloured or distorted. He wrote an account of them, but 'twas nothing but the account of his miserable feelings.....

Smollett's *Travels Through France and Italy* is still a classic of its type in English and an essential part of his canon.

In May 1766 he was on his travels for his health once more, visiting Bath. The spa treatment seemed to improve the muscle tone of his limbs. He wrote to Dr John Moore on 13 November 1765:

......If I was a galley slave, and kept to hard labour for two or three years, I believe I should recover my health entirely. The Bath water agrees with me wonderfully well; and upon the whole, I am so well at present that some of my friends declare they never saw me look better; but I will venture to say I am not above half as big as I was when you saw me last. To tell you the truth, I look upon my being alive as a sort of resuscitation, for last year I thought myself in the last stage of consumption....

In the late spring of 1766 the Smolletts travelled to Scotland, where they visited their remaining relatives and friends in Edinburgh and Glasgow. Among these was Smollett's cousin, James Smollett, who was a Judge of the Commissary Court. Tobias was heir-presumptive to his estates, and no doubt he kept his notorious temper when in discourse with him... His health continued to decline, and in spite of his previous experiences when canvassing favours from the great, he hoped that through friends he might obtain the patronage of someone well placed in the establishment who could grant him a consulship somewhere warm. Letters written during the late summer of 1767 show endeavours made on Smollett's behalf, but to no avail. As John Moore recorded of this period:

> These applications were fruitless. Dr Smollett had never spanielled ministers: he could not endure the insolence of office, or stoop to cultivate the favour of any person merely on account of his power: and beside, he was a man of genius....

He was now resolved, whatever the personal cost, to leave for the continent. He travelled with his wife to Lucca, then to Pisa and ultimately, to Leghorn. He rented a villa near Antignano, overlooking the sea. Before he departed he delivered himself of his most scathing and most notorious satire, the still neglected *The History and Adventures of an Atom* which he published in Dublin and in Edinburgh. He left for Italy in the Autumn of 1768; the satire was published in the following April. The Atom of the title was enclosed in a grain of rice in Japan and, after passing through various vicissitudes (dysentery, manure, raised in a vegetable, eaten in a salad, brought to England, eaten by a duck etc.) it finishes up in the pineal gland of one Nathaniel Peacock. The Atom tells Nathaniel its adventures as well as the recent socio-political history of Japan. The book has attracted little comment, and is among the few of Smollett's which has not been re-edited for modern times - probably because of the complexity of its topical allusions. Its satirical portraits possess vigour, and it would well repay the study it has not yet received.

In the Autumn of 1770 he was composing his masterpiece, *The*

Expedition of Humphry Clinker. Smollett, as a practitioner of the early, formative years of the English novel, had always been interested in the possibilities of form. This novel, like Richardson's *Pamela* and *Clarissa*, was written in the form of a series of letters. It was published in June 1771. The story is by no means complex, but the method by which it is told is rich, subtle and extremely human. It narrates the adventures of Matthew Bramble, an elderly Welsh valetudinarian who travels for the sake of his health (which is not so bad as he likes to maintain) together with his family through England and Scotland. There are notable set pieces at Bath, Bristol, London, Harrogate, Durham, Edinburgh and the Highlands. Accompanying Matthew are his sister Tabitha, an elderly husband - seeking harridan; Jerry, his nephew, a young gad-about town, and his sister, Lydia. The maid, Win, and Humphry, a young ostler whom they encounter and who becomes their postilion, are among the other characters. There are various humorous and amorous entanglements. Tabitha is married off, Lydia falls for a young nobleman in disguise as an actor and Humphry is revealed as Matthew Bramble's natural son and marries Win Jenkins, the servant girl. The novel is outstanding for its brilliant portrayal of contemporary social *mores* and for the enrichment and wit of the narrative told — as it is — in a series of letters from these various characters to sundry friends and relatives, with the consequent opportunity, exploited by the genius of Smollett, to display several points of view of characters and incidents. Never as popular as *Clarissa*, *Humphry Clinker* improved upon it technically and, of course, where Richardson had been (in Coleridge's words) "oozy", Smollett was, despite his famous irascibility, tolerant and humane.

Tobias Smollett died at Leghorn on 17 September 1771. He was fifty. The Italian physician who attended him during his last illness soon became aware of his irascible, paranoid temperament. He expressed his state of mind in the opening letter (dated 23 June 1763 from Boulogne) of *Travels Through France and Italy* (1766):

You knew, and pitied my situation, traduced by malice, persecuted by faction, abandoned by false patrons, and overwhelmed by the sense of a domestic calamity, which it was not in the power of fortune to repair....

It is understandable. He knew his ability, and knew how hard he had laboured. But he always felt that as an outsider — as an ambitious literary Scotsman in the metropolis — he had never achieved acceptance. He had not succeeded in getting himself properly acknowledged, or quite admitted to the inner circle. Life had given him other blows, most profoundly, the death of his young daughter. He had always struggled to make ends meet. Had he lived a few more years he would have inherited the estate of Bonhill — worth £1,000 a year — from his cousin, James Smollett. He came to London with little except his ill-fated, and, it must be conceded, worthless, drama *The Regicide*. By the time of his death he had become an established professional writer. In his last novel he offered a brief portrait of himself. He might well have described himself in the words he uses in *Humphry Clinker*, as "an author of the first distinction". There should be no dispute about that. But there still is. The purpose of this essay is to establish the case for his true greatness, and to demonstrate his proper place in the history of our literature. He was a pioneer of professional authorship, a founding father of the English novel and the creator of at least one immortal work. That is the nature of his distinction.

II WORKS : SMOLLETT AND THE NOVEL
The Adventures of Roderick Random
The Adventures of Peregrine Pickle

Smollett was a man of very agreeable conversation and of much genuine humour; and, though not a profound scholar, possessed a philosophical mind, and was capable of making the soundest observations on human life, and of discussing the excellence or seeing the ridicule of every character he met with..... (Alexander Carlyle: The Autobiography of Dr Alexander Carlyle of Inveresk 1722-1805, 1860, edited by J.H.Burton. 1910)

Beginnings of the English Novel

Tobias Smollett was a founding father of the English novel. The majority of his miscellaneous bread-and-butter journalism and popular history is now forgotten, but three of his novels - *Roderick Random*, *Peregrine Pickle* and *Humphry Clinker* - continue to be read valued and enjoyed. Their enduring popularity is testified by to the fact that they can be had in paperback editions well over two hundred years since their author's death. They are, in addition, landmarks in the development of the English novel. It is often asserted, not unreasonably, that the English novel "began in the 18th century"; but we need to remind ourselves just what this "beginning" actually was. Daniel Defoe published the three works we collectively know by the title of "Robinson Crusoe" in 1720. *Moll Flanders* and *Colonel Jacque* appeared in 1722. But are these works "novels"? There continues to be a debate, much of it sterile, as to what constitutes a novel.

The Craze for Romances

The Elizabethans enjoyed narrative prose fiction. This category embraces prose works usually called "romances". These romances dealt with marvellous, extraordinary, fantastic events which take place in exotic locations. The main ingredients were invariably a selection from a limited shopping list: they include elements of love, separation and reunion, intermingled with adventure, spectacle, derring-do and enchantment. Such popular tales were ransacked by dramatists looking for useful plots - Shakespeare, of course, among them e.g. Robert Greene's *Pandosto* 1588, - *The Winter's Tale*.

The craze for romance was furthered by numerous translations of French, Spanish and Italian popular fiction. It was the mad craze for fanciful yarns of enchanted islands, magicians, endangered maidens, virtuous knights, cunning squires, enchanted landscapes and brave steeds which inspired Cervantes to compose the first part of *Don Quixote* (1605). But the craze for romances continued throughout the 17th century; if anything, the works grew more fantastic. Honore d'Urfé's immensely popular and influential *L'Astrée* (1607-27) and Madeline de Scudery's *Le Grand Cyrus* (1649-53) had their imitators in Britain (such as Mrs Aphra Behn) and produced a vogue for the exotic and extravagant theatrical spectacular entertainment which was so outstanding a feature of the Restoration stage. The vogue for the exotic was further encouraged by the immense popularity of *The Arabian Nights Entertainment*, given European circulation in Antoine Galland's French version (1704-1717), put into English almost immediately.

Socio-Economic and Political Changes and their effect on culture

The ethos of public affairs and the socio-economic structures of society were changing. The English Civil War - which was, among other more complex things, a public challenge to the Divine Right of Kings - signalled a new social era.

The Commonwealth ended with the Restoration of Charles II, but eighteen years later his brother James II was driven from the throne in a bloodless revolution. The nature of the settlement parliament negotiated for William and Mary, the succession of the House of Hanover, and the domination of national politics by the Whig party under Walpole for the first part of the century demonstrated the growing new strength and importance of the land-owning, trading, commercial and merchant class.

The wealth of the nation depended more and more upon banking, financial services, trade and manufacture. Such fundamental developments in the economic basis of society showed themselves in the concomitant ideological and cultural changes. In 18th century Britain there were two particularly significant cultural manifestations in drama. *The Beggar's Opera* (1728) by John Gay, and *The London Merchant, or the History of George Barnwell* (1731) by George Lillo. John Gay's ballad opera of the life and love-tangles of its highwayman hero, set to popular tunes, traditional airs and ballads, challenged the supremacy of the aristocratic fashion for Italian opera. George Lillo's play, based on a traditional ballad story of the corruption of a sound young man by an ambitious woman who incites him to murder his old uncle for his money, first produced at Drury Lane in 1731, ushered in the new domestic middle-class drama, set not in lavish palaces or exotic locations, but in recognisable everyday locations. *George Barnwell* was immensely popular, and frequently imitated.

Everyday Realities and the Novel

The English novel emerged to feed this new appetite for the mundane and common-sensical. What was wanted, it seems, was something which more believably examined everyday realities and in a relatively 'ordinary' manner. Samuel Richardson, with *Pamela* and *Clarissa* already behind him, wrote to Miss Muso on 5 October 1752: "....what a deuce, do you think I am writing a Romance? Don't you see that I am copying Nature....." Richardson's heroine, the over-virtuous Pamela, rejects the nonsense world featured in the romances offered her by her mistress. She finds these fictions improbable, the adventures ridiculous, humiliating of her true nature and unlikely to teach her anything worthwhile about life:

.....there were very few novels and romances that my lady would permit me to read; and those I did, gave me no great pleasure; for either they dealt so much in the marvellous and improbable, or were so unnaturally inflaming to the passions, and so full of love and intrigue, that most of them seemed calculated to fire the imagination, rather than to inform the judgement...... .And what is the instruction that can be gathered from such pieces, for the conduct of common life? (Samuel Richardson: *Pamela*, or *Virtue Rewarded* 1740, Part II, Letter 102).

The literary revolution achieved by Samuel Richardson, Henry Fielding and Tobias Smollett was sufficiently realised by 1750 as to receive the imprimatur of official recognition by Samuel Johnson:

The works of fiction with which the present generation seems more particularly delighted are such as exhibit life in its true state, diversified only by accidents that daily happen in the world, and influenced by passions and qualities which are really to be found in conversing with mankind.

This kind of writing may be termed not improperly the comedy of romance, and is to be conducted nearly by the rules of comic poetry. Its province is to bring about natural events by easy means, and to keep up curiosity without the help of wonder: it is therefore precluded from the machines and expedients of the heroic romance, and can neither employ giants to snatch away a lady from the nuptial rites, nor knights to bring her back from captivity: it can neither bewilder its personages in deserts nor lodge them in imaginary castles..... (Samuel Johnson: The Rambler, Number 4, Saturday 31 March 1750)

Smollett and the Emergence of the Novel

Smollett's role in the revolutionary process which brought the modern novel into being was highly individual. One curious fact about Smollett's work so obvious that it is almost invariably overlooked is that he produced no prentice work. Unlike, say, Charles Dickens, who produced sketches and short stories before venturing into anything which might be regarded as a novel, Smollett (after his unsuccessful attempts to get his drama staged) launched straight into novel writing. There had been nothing quite like *Roderick Random* before. Smollett had already seen and experienced enough to provide the basic stuff of a novel. But what of the form in which he cast it? The term *picaresque novel* comes all too easily to mind, but what actually is implied?

Smollett's first novel is unlike its immediate British precursors. Richardson's *Pamela, or Virtue Rewarded* had appeared at the end of 1740. Written as a series of letters from a virtuous fifteen year-old servant girl, it told the story of her sturdy resistance to all the attempts on her honour by the young man of the household, who eventually kidnaps her and attempts her seduction. She, in turn, attempts to reform him. Henry Fielding had parodied this tale in his *The History of the Adventures of Joseph Andrews and his friend, Mr Abraham Adams* early in 1742. The hero is supposed to be Pamela's brother, and is similarly exposed to the wicked intentions of his employers. He is a virtuous young footman, and is compelled to repulse the amorous advances of his mistress, her ladyship. He runs away to be with his beloved, his true love, Fanny Goodwill. Hero and heroine are set upon by thieves, but rescued by Parson Adams. After sundry plot twists and adventures they are united in matrimony. What had commenced as a parody of the smug self-conscious virtuism of *Pamela* became in Fielding's hands a rumbustious comic novel of Hanoverian England. In the following year Fielding published *The Life of Jonathan Wild the Great*, presented as the biography of the fence, informer and thief-taker, Jonathan Wild, who had been hanged in 1725. The novel is, in fact, a political satire on the Whig Prime Minister, Robert Walpole, who maintained himself in office by an elaborate system of prefer-ment and back-handers, bribing enemies and selling friends when he considered it expedient. There is not much in English that might have influenced Smollett except, possibly, some of the Cervantes-like episodes in *Joseph Andrews.*

Smollett and the Picaresque

Smollett's first novel emerges as an entirely new kind of narrative prose fiction, and in the Preface he goes to some length to explain what he is trying to do.

This novel, he claims, is intended to be satiric as well as enter-taining. The satire is to be introduced occasionally into "an interesting story" in which familiar scenes are to be represented "in an uncommon and amusing point of view" invested with novelty but yet remaining true to nature. The book is constructed to instruct and entertain:

> The reader gratifies his curiosity, in pursuing the adventures of a person in whose favour he is prepossessed; he espouses his cause, he sympathises with him in distress, his indignation is heated against the authors of his calamity; the humane passions are inflamed; the contrast between dejected virtue, and insulting vice, appears with greater aggravation, and every impression having a double force upon the imagination, the memory retains the circumstance, and the heart improves by the example. The attention is not tired with a bar Catalogue of characters, but agreeably diverted with all the variety of invention; and the vicissitudes of life appear in their peculiar circumstances, opening up ample field for wit and humour. (Smollett: Preface to *Roderick Random* 1748)

Smollett then adds the by now familiar attack on Romances as performances filled with "monstrous hyperboles", which taxed the credulity and wonder of readers, with ludicrous, extravagant and unnatural ingredients. He was actively engaged on his translation of Cervantes' *Don Quixote* at this stage in his career: it was published in 1755. He pays tribute to its author, stating that it took the genius of Cervantes to take the Romance form and, in *Don Quixote*, produce a comic romance which tended to reform the world and make it a better place, by pointing out human folly.

He refers to "other Spanish and French authors" among them Le Sage, the author of *Gil Blas*, and acknowledges the influence these works have had on him. The Spanish stories he refers to are the Spanish picaresque novels of the 16th and 17th centuries, such as the anonymous *Lazarillo de Tormes* (one of the most widely read prose works of the 16th century), *Guzman d'Alfarache* by Mateo Aleman, *El coloquio de los perros* and *Rinconete y Cortadillo* (*Novelas Ejemplares*) by Cervantes and Quevedo's *Historia de la vida del Buscon*. English translations of these were much read throughout the 18th century.

These original Spanish picaresque novels retailed the life and adventures of a rogue, trickster or con-man (*picaro* means approximately, a rogue) on his journey through life. He is almost invariably a likeable, rather than villainous rascal - one with quick wits who may be seen to be exploiting the selfish ways of his superiors which are invariably the subject of satire. For some reason or other — the loss of parents, sudden poverty, illegitimacy — this hero is cast out into the world to make his own way, to struggle against an unaccommodating society, and to trick and cheat his way through life. He is usually accompanied by a loyal comic serving man. The hero is headstrong and passionate, whereas the serving man is a natural philosopher and combines peasant cunning with an ability to see things as they really are. This basic set of relationships owes everything to the Quixote-Panza relationship: however Quixote is not a *picaro* but a poetic and romantic idealist gifted with a sort of innocent way of deviating into sense. The *picaro's* adventures are harum-scarum, random, episodic, involving plenty of ridiculous situations and escapades which require him to live on his wits. He is usually saved from serious troubles by his serving man. Things turn out well in the end and, his fortune secure, the hero marries and settles down (his servant usually marries a young maidservant).

Elements in this tradition were taken over by Defoe in *Moll Flanders* and *Colonel Jaque*; but by the time the picaresque tradition fully emerges in English literature the hero is less of a rogue and more of a high-spirited prankster, let loose in the world to have his rough edges smoothed off in preparation for a mature and settled life. But the basic plot outline - a series of loosely assembled adventures, connected solely on the basis that they all happen to the same character, who is invariably accompanied by a comic alter-ego - is used by Smollett and Fielding and, much later, imitated by Dickens. You can sense the prototype behind such figures as Pickwick and Sam Weller; Martin Chuzzlewit and Mark Tapley.

From the very beginning the picaresque tradition was firmly rooted in the endeavour to write narrative prose fiction that was believable, true to life.

Smollett's View of the Novel

Smollett described the novel type he believed he had evolved in the *Dedication* to his third novel, *The Adventures of Ferdinand Count Fathom*:

> A novel is a large diffused picture, comprehending the characters of life, disposed in different groups, and exhibited in various attitudes, for the purpose of an uniformed plan, and general occurrence, to which every individual figure is subservient. But this plan cannot be executed with propriety, probability, or success, without a principal personage to attract the attention, unite the incidents, unwind the clue of the labyrinth, and at last close the scene, by virtue of his own importance. (Smollett: Dedication to *Ferdinand Count Fathom* 1753)

There we have in clear outline as good a description of the picaresque novel as one could wish - a series of rambling adventures which are held together and made credible, happen to the same leading character, set in a wide range of social contexts, which exhibit life in all its varieties. The whole apparently random sequence to receive a dénouement at the conclusion of the novel. We have further insight into Smollett's thinking about plot structure in a review, almost certainly by him, which appeared in the *Critical Review* in January 1763. Implied throughout this critical discussion of a new novel are a series of basic assumptions which collectively define what Smollett clearly thought a picaresque novel should be. It is a notice of a new novel, *The Peregrinations of Jeremiah Grant Esquire, the West Indian*. Smollett notes that the structure is loose and unrestrained; the series of adventures is held together by the leading character, to whom all other characters are subservient; in selecting his incidents the novelist must always take nature as his guide; and that the work should have a guiding principle or moral theme to bind the elements together. In reviewing *Jeremiah Grant* Smollett says that mere observation of nature is not enough. Modern novels "deal chiefly among the familiar scenes of life, and bring to the view characters which we every day view in nature; for this reason it seems to be an easy species of writing, and encourages many to turn authors whose talents are not suited to the task...."

The aim of a picaresque novel was to improve mankind by laughing at folly, but this should be done without undue impropriety. A picaresque novel should not be too extravagant, otherwise readers will not believe it. Additionally, whatever happens to the hero, and whatever he does, he should still remain a sympathetic character. His main criticism of *Jeremiah Grant* is that it seems to have no moral intention whatsoever, no purpose except to entertain. The question is, Smollett asks: "whether a dull recital of uninteresting facts can afford any entertainment to the public, or be any use to the community". A vast variety of incidents in themselves is of no use, unless these incidents have some reason for happening. He narrates the wretched story, which certainly seemed to include every possible picaresque cliché - loss of money, whores, begging, life in the army, re-united friends, nuns in convents, capture by pirates, rescue by Jack Tars, affairs with society ladies, and eventually the hero's marriage to "a young lady of whom he had been formerly enamoured". Smollett comments on this ragbag: "such are the outlines of this performance, in which we cannot say there is a want of variety..." There are serious flaws in the novel. It is extravagant beyond belief. Of the episode in which Jeremiah gets shot through the head and lives, Smollett comments: "this circumstance calculated to imply that there were no brains in the skull, a truth which perhaps we should have discovered from other parts of the work, even if this hint had not been given..." The entire string of adventures he finds stretch credulity beyond the bounds of endurance: "his final settlement in life is much more comfortable than poetic justice would allow to a character of his stamp; for it is such as can never entitle him to the respect of the sensible reader...." Jeremiah Grant in Smollett's view is a thoroughly unsympathetic character:

The follies of Mr Grant excite contempt rather than laughter; and his distress is of such a nature that hardly moves our compassion....It requires the art of a master to exhibit a character in the lowest scenes of indigence, still an object of attention and esteem. (Smollett: Critical Review, January 1763 pp. 14 ff.)

The Adventures of Roderick Random

In his review of *Jeremiah Grant* Smollett presents his understanding of the principles of the picaresque novel. Smollett's first novel, *Roderick Random*, conforms to these principles very closely. The novelist writes in his *Preface* that he made his hero a Scot because:

> I could at a small expense bestow on him such education as I thought the dignity of his birth and character required, which could not possibly be obtained in England, by such slender means as the nature of my plan would afford.

Further, he could represent simplicity of manners in a remote part of the kingdom, which he could not do had he sited the novel nearer the metropolis. Lastly, he says, the Scots have a great inclination to be travellers and wanderers, and he could consequently locate the various adventures in different locations. All these considerations are stressed: they would clearly render the novel more believable.

Many of the opening sections of *Roderick Random* are autobiographical. They burn with Smollett's personal feelings. Into these pages he pours his anger and resentment at the rigid and unfair social system which had so firmly closed its doors against him when he first came from Scotland to London as an ambitious young man sincerely convinced of his own worth and ability. Roderick is a similarly hardheaded and ambitious Scot, convinced of his true merits and angry with the world for not recognising them. The theme of the novel is clearly stated in the Preface: Smollett wished to represent "modest merit struggling with every difficulty to which a friendless orphan is exposed, from his own want of experience, as well as from selfishness, envy, malice, and base indifference of mankind". He comes to London with his schoolfriend, Strap, and a letter of introduction which he believes will secure him the appointment as a naval surgeon. Such ambitions, he is to learn, are very expensive. The path to preferment must be perforce eased with ample funds. Passing the examination by the Navy board involves bribery at all levels, even paying the servants who open the door for him:

> Next day we returned to the Navy Office, where, after being called before the Board, and questioned about the place of my nativity and education, they ordered a letter to be made out for me, which, upon paying half a crown to the clerk, I received, and delivered into the hands of the clerk at Surgeons' Hall, together with a shilling for his trouble in registering my name. By this time my whole stock was diminished to two shillings, and I saw not the least prospect of relief, even for present subsistence, much less to pay the fees at Surgeons' Hall for my examination..... (*Roderick Random*, Chapter XVI)

Roderick has the mortification to see young men appointed simply because they had the wherewithal to dispense. He borrows money and takes the examination, readily answering the series of medical and surgical questions the panel put to him:

> In less than a quarter of an hour I was called in....received my qualification sealed up, and was ordered to pay five shillings. I laid down my half guinea upon the table, and stood some time, until one of them bade me begone; to this I replied, "I will, when I have got my change"; upon which another threw me five shillings and six pence.... I was afterwards obliged to give three shillings and six pence to the beadles, and a shilling to an old woman who swept the hall.....(ibid XVII)

This is by no means the end of the capital outlay for his putative naval career. Roderick's funds rapidly diminish, and he reaches the conclusion that his only means of survival must lie in service either with the army or the navy. While considering the choice, he falls victim to the press-gang and is tumbled about H.M.S.Thunder and serves in the disastrous expedition to Cartegena in the West Indies in the war with Spain. The shipboard episodes, (Chapters XXIV to XXXVII are among the most brilliant pages Smollett ever wrote) must have struck readers as reality considerably heightened. Yet research tends to support the novelist's portrait of naval service at this time. The food was appalling, consisting mainly of salt meat, biscuit, cheese, beer and dried fish. As ships were manned with the dregs from the nation's gaols and men press-ganged into service, discipline was harsh. The tyrannical Captain Oakum is shocked to learn so many crew reported sick and resolves "there'll be no sickness aboard the Thunder". In a scene much in the style of *The Good Soldier Schweik* he orders the sick on parade, with the ship's medical officer looking on:

> The first who came under his cognisance, was a poor fellow just freed from fever...he could hardly stand.....Mr Mackshane.....protested he was as well as any man in the world; and the captain delivered him over to the boatswain's mate, with orders that he should receive a round dozen at the gangway immediately, for counterfeiting himself sick when he was not; but before the discipline could be administered, the man dropt down on the deck and might well nigh have perished.....The next...laboured under a quartan ague....he was declared fit for duty, and turned over to the boatswain; but being resolved to disgrace the doctor, died upon the forecastle next day....The third complained of a pleuretic stitch, and spitting blood, for which doctor Mackshane prescribed exercise at the pump...in less than half an hour, he was suffocated with a deluge of blood that issued from his lungs. ..(Chapter XXVII)

The dreadful catalogue continues. Disease was rampant, and the living conditions were cramped and insanitary. Sickness prevailed. Medical treatment was crude and brutal. Roderick is shocked at these conditions. He is amazed not so much that so many sailors die, but that so many seem able to recover. In the sick bay he sees:

> .....about fifty miserable distempered wretches, suspended in rows, so huddled upon one another, that not more than fourteen inches of space was allotted for each with his bed and bedding; and deprived of the light of day, as well as of fresh air; breathing but a noisome atmosphere....devoured with vermin hatched in the filth that surrounded them, and destitute of every convenience necessary for people in that helpless condition....

At Cartegena, the wet season brings about a change in the

atmosphere which has a deleterious effect on the health of the seamen:

> The change of atmosphere, occasioned by this phenomenon, conspired, with the stench that surrounded us, the heat of the climate, our own constitutions impoverished by bad provisions, and our despair, to introduce the bilious fever among us, which raged with such violence, that three fourths of those whom it invaded died.....(ibid Chapter XXXIV)

Roderick himself falls ill. (Naval records disclose that Smollett was ill himself during his service on this expedition. H.M.S.*Chichester's* muster records his pay deductions). It is interesting to note that Smollett incorporates descriptions of these military and naval operations in *An Account of the Expedition against Cartegena*, published in 1756, and that they are very similar to the account in *Roderick Random*. Modern scholarship has confirmed the accuracy of his accounts of naval conditions and treatment of the sick and wounded. R.S.Allison comments: "Tobias Smollett, who served as a surgeon's mate... in the year 1739, has always been accused of exaggerating ... the conditions that existed at that time, but he was probably not far from the truth...."(*The Sea Diseases of the Royal Navy*, 1925) and he specifically links the work of such reformers as Dr James Lind (*An Essay on the Most Effectual Means of Preserving the Health of Seamen in the Royal Navy: Dissertation on Fevers & Infections, together with Observations on the Jail Fever* 1774) with Smollett's satiric portrayal of shipboard conditions.

Roderick stays for a while in the West Indies and returns penniless to London. Smollett, having scrutinised life in the navy, then turn his attention to the social scene ashore. When Roderick takes a job as a footman, he falls in love with Narcissa, his mistress' beautiful daughter. Next he is captured by smugglers and taken to France, where he joins the Regiment of Picardy. His friend Strap turns up and the two team up and return to England. After various shifts — including gambling and social-climbing — have failed to get him into the kind of life he thinks he should be enjoying, he seeks a government post through the cultivation of various aristocratic patrons. These pages assemble a brilliant picture of England dominated by the powerful Whig magnates. Once again, modern scholarship establishes that what might have seemed exaggerated to Smollett's readers was in fact a valid but of course, satirical account of the way the system worked.

Roderick attempts to begin his career in public office by ingratiating himself with two young lords, Straddle and Swillpot. Through them he is put in contact with the powerful Lord Strutwell. He eggs him on with various nods, winks and promises ("How would you like to cross the sea, as secretary to an embassy?") and gradually fleeces him of everything he has, including his watch. Roderick finally learns that Strutwell is a notorious homosexual rake who has other plans for Roderick than advancing his career.

This entrée to high society having failed, Roderick then embarks on social adventures and amorous escapades in Bath. He is eventually thrown into the Marshalsea prison for a debt to his tailor. Here he learns the sad story of Melopoyn, who had composed a tragedy which he then failed to get performed upon the stage because he was unable to find a patron (this parallels Smollett's own misadventures with his tragedy, *The Regicide*, and the insolence of his patrons). He is rescued from prison by his sea-faring uncle, Tom Bowling, who has just done rather well from some privateering. He accompanies Bowling on an expedition to South America, makes a fortune, finds his long-lost father, returns to England and marries his beloved Narcissa.

Smollett's achievement in this first novel was to take a now established Spanish form, as further refined by Le Sage (but Le Sage had given his characters Spanish names and chose Spain as his setting), and presses it to serve satiric purposes of his own, presenting a colourful, convincing and rich portrait of several layers of British society in the late 1730's and early 1740's - the twilight of Walpole's reign over a thriving and over-ripe nation. He showed his readers the society in which they lived as they had not seen it before. True, Smollett owed much to Defoe, but, he differed in two important respects: his scenes have an extra validity because of the personal experience invested in them; and he was more deliberately comic. Additionally, the element of self-satire in *Roderick Random* should not be underestimated. He mocks himself, for example, in the figure of the would be tragedian Melopoyn.

The Adventures of Peregrine Pickle

Smollett's next novel, *The Adventures of Peregrine Pickle*, appeared in 1751. Superficially, it is of much the same mixture as *Roderick Random*. But in fact the emphasis is different. In his first novel the perspective is essentially that of one from the lower end of society trying to break in. *Peregrine Pickle* focuses severely on the essential shallowness and triviality of high society. Although the plot seems to resemble the traditional picaresque mode, Peregrine is no picaro. He is well born and financially stable. He has no need to beg and trick his way through life. Unlike Roderick, he is not an outsider seeking to gain entry to the inside. Peregrine moves naturally and smoothly within the inner circles of well-to-do society. The theme is the vacuousness of those who inhabit those circles, and their power to corrode and corrupt the human spirit. Even the notorious interpolated *Memoirs of a Lady of Quality* contribute to this theme. Pride and arrogance leave Peregrine open to corruption of this tainted society, but he is purged and achieves personal salvation.

The danger for a novelist attempting to handle such themes lies in the ease with which the sleaze and immoral aspects of the social scenes thus depicted may be made to seem racy, sophisticated or attractive, and virtue seem correspondingly smug or dull. By making much of Peregrine's early personal behaviour rough and heartless, and many of his actions motivated by a less than admirable pride, Smollett - once again, self-critically - evades the pitfalls.

Peregrine's pride is shown in several ways - extravagance, love of admiration, shallow ambition and materialism. As in Dickens's later treatment of a very similar personality, Pip in *Great Expectations*,

Peregrine fails to recognise his true friends, and trusts falsity, because his standards are based on money values. His father sets him a bad example, and he in turn inherited it from his father. Grandfather Pickle lost his substance in speculation. The novel's opening paragraph gives out this theme. Grandfather's dying words strike the keynote: "....imitate my industry and adhere to my maxims until you make up the deficiency, which sum is considerably less than fifteen thousand pounds..." Peregrine has reached the end of his spiritual journey when, at the end of the novel, with the words "Damn the money!" Pipes throws the money into the fire. After a life dominated by money values, of mistaking appearances for realities, Peregrine now realises that money for its own sake has no real value. The theme is constant. The society through which Peregrine moves, and in which he initially hopes to achieve such triumph, is dominated by such values. This is the significance of the beautiful episode of the Nymph of the Road, whom he metamorphoses into a "Fine Lady" and passes off in high society, (Chapter XCV). The appearance/reality theme, social snobbery, and gullibility are constantly rehearsed in *Peregrine Pickle*: false conceptions of honour, phoney knowledge, quackery manifested as professional expertise, infidelity, lust mistaken for love, social snobbery in Bath, legal chicanery, sharping of sundry kinds, hype and publicity, the shallow world of horse-racing and politics. He falls in love with the beautiful Emilia Gauntlet, and attempts to woo her. After he has been further corrupted by high life at home and abroad, marriage with her seems rather less than desirable; but he intends to enjoy her nevertheless. She perceives his shallowness for what it is. His attempt to buy her affections with jewelry and physically to seduce her are the low water-mark of his moral odyssey. It is prison, as a microcosm of the world outside, which finally purges Peregrine. (This, too, finds its echoes in recurring configurations of experience in Dickens). With an almost modernist touch, filled with irony, Smollett underlines these themes when his hero is in prison:

I might here, in imitation of some celebrated writers, furnish out a page or two, with the reflections he made upon the instability of human affairs, the treachery of the world, and the temerity of youth; and endeavour to decoy the reader into a smile, by some quaint observation of my own, touching the sagacious moraliser. But, besides that I look upon the practice as an impertinent anticipation of the peruser's thoughts, I have too much matter of importance upon my hands, to give the reader the least reason to believe that I am driven to such paltry shifts, in order to eke out the volume. (Chapter CV)

Instead, Smollett demonstrates that in prison, a world without money, real humanity can at least show itself. Peregrine can no longer employ his serving man, so he is dismissed. But the loyal Pipes offers his master the benefit of his savings. Peregrine refuses — and it is at this moment that, as Pipes throws the money in the flames, Peregrine's heart is at last reached: "...he could scarce suppress his sorrow in the presence of Pipes, and soon as he was gone, it vented itself in tears". (CV) The personal histories of various prison companions further serve to drive home the false world of society:

No man scrupled to own the nature of the debt fore which he was confined, unless it happened to be some piddling affair; but, on the contrary, boasted of the importance of the sum, as a circumstance that implied his having been a person of consequence in life; and he who had made the most remarkable escapes from bailiffs, was looked upon as a man of superior genius and address. (Chapter CV)

A friend from his earlier life, Gauntlet, comes to see him and offers him help. Significantly he does not offer him money, but friendship. Peregrine is now showing physical signs of the impact of his misfortunes, but, above that, he is now able to see matters clearly, and to long for the true and fulfilling things that a wholesome life can offer, such as domesticity, simple routines, partnership, love and affection, making and growing things. Those are the very things he had previously scorned. The threads of the novel are swiftly pulled together by the traditional means of inherited wealth, forgiveness and reconciliation. Peregrine and Emilia are united.

III WORKS:
The Adventures of Ferdinand Count Fathom;
The Life and Adventures of Sir Launcelot Greaves

Smollett's next two novels are by no means as complex. *Ferdinand Count Fathom* appeared two years after *Pickle*. It is one of Smollett's least satisfying novels, but not without interest. It is set in the early 18th century. The hero is the son of a camp follower in the War of the Spanish Succession. He has no right to the title, but calls himself Count. The plot is of the picaresque sort, and, such as it is, recounts a series of Ferdinand's villainies which include theft, seduction, attempted seduction and fraud. Like Peregrine, he too heads for prison, but his repentance is too impetuous and conventional to be as convincing. Such interest as this novel continues to hold is to be found in the colourful portrait of the social whirl of the day — gambling, moneylending, sexual dalliance, quackery and the demi-monde.

Sir Launcelot Greaves was serialised in 1760. In structure it appears to be based on the comic-epic introduced into English fiction by Henry Fielding in *Joseph Andrews* (1742) That is to say, it is the comic equivalent of epic — the story of hero against adversities in which his integrity is severely tested, but instead of wars, battles and conflicts we have rough-and-tumble, escapades and amusing situations ending, not with catastrophe and tragedy, but with reconciliation and happiness. The hero of this strange novel is an aristocrat who forgoes his inheritance in order to put right the many wrongs he discerns in modern society. The theme of simple and eccentric saints, struggling to assert themselves in a world which does not heed them, points towards Samuel Pickwick; and Dickens did read the novel with particular interest. As well as the reforming knight errantry of Cervantes' mythic prototype, Smollett also works hard at ironic associations with Arthurian idealism. Greaves proclaims himself a Knight Errant to the amazed customers of a modern English hostelry:

The good company wonders, no doubt, to see a man cased in armour, such as hath been for above a whole century disused in this and every other country of Europe; and perhaps they will be still more surprised, when they hear that man profess himself a novitiate of that military order, which hath of old been distinguished in Great Britain, as well as through Christendom, by the name of Knights Errant. Yes, gentlemen, in that painful and thorny path of toil and danger I have begun my career, a candidate for honest fame; determined, as far as in me lies, to honour and assert the efforts of virtue; to combat vice in all her forms, redress injuries, chastise oppression, protect the helpless and forlorn, relieve the indigent, exert my best endeavours in the cause of innocence and beauty, and dedicate my talents, such as they are, to the service of my country.....(Chapter II)

The social satire in this novel is aimed at the socio-economic and political state of the nation. Hanoverian Britain had been plunged into serious debt by the long continental and colonial war which began in 1756 and lasted until 1763. Among the targets Smollett assaults are the government, the establishment and several of the professions (priests, physicians and lawyers in particular). These satiric attacks are draped on to the strange adventures prompted by Sir Launcelot's disappointment in love. There is some familial legal chicanery. Madness is one of the more intriguing of the themes which holds this strange book together. The theme of madness is examined in several respects. It is explored from the hero's own standpoint as well as in an exploration of society's treatment of its lunatics. Over and above this is the ultimate question of society's own sanity. Smollett demonstrates that the kingdom is full of mountebanks, in religion, medicine, law, politics, patriotism:

....quacks in government; high German quacks that have blistered, sweated, bled and purged the nation into atrophy. But this is not all; they have not only evacuated her into a consumption, but they have intoxicated her brain, and until she is become delirious....(Ibid Chapter X)

At the end of the novel the mysteries are unravelled, Sir Launcelot is restored to his inheritance and reunited with his beloved. His mission over, he sheds his armour - as the perfect and uninterrupted felicity of the knight and his consort is celebrated:

> ....as far as their example and influence could extend. They were admired, esteemed, and applauded by every person of taste, sentiment, and benevolence; at the same time beloved, revered, and almost adored by the common people, among whom they suffered not the merciless hand of indigence or misery to seize one single sacrifice. (Chapter the Last)

IV WORKS :
The Expedition of Humphry Clinker

Smollett's last novel, *The Expedition of Humphry Clinker* (1771) is his masterpiece, and certainly among the finest of all English novels. Written as it was, after a period of serious illness, it is certainly also an extraordinarily generous work, one of reconciliation which makes a fitting close to Smollett's career as a master novelist. It sublimely balances and complements his first novel, *Roderick Random*. *Humphry Clinker* is, like *Roderick Random*, the story of a provincial Briton who leaves his native land and travels the country. Matthew Bramble travels, not from Scotland, but from Wales. Nevertheless, as was the case with Roderick, Smollett uses this "outsider" character as a means of commenting on the condition of the nation through which he travels. The novel is the story of the Bramble family's journey, but further, it is a summing up of Smollett's final vision of the United Kingdom. The plot is simplicity itself. But the Book's richness and humanity lies in its telling.

Matthew Bramble of Brambleton Hall is a well-to-do land-owning squire, a valetudinarian who travels for the sake of his health. He is a hypochondriac, but his irascible temper hides a heart of gold. He has but little faith in medical men (a constant theme in Smollett's fiction: a kind of ironic self-undermining which is one measure of the true writer) but resolves to take their advice and visit Bath to take the waters.

This journey for the sake of his health turns out to be a family odyssey. He takes with him his unmarried sister, the harridan Tabitha Bramble, who has not entirely given up hope of finding a husband. She takes with her the chattering, gushing Winifred Jenkins, her maid-servant. Also in their company are Matthew's nephew and niece, Jerry Melford and his sister Lydia. Jerry is a young student, Lydia an impres-sionable young girl who continues to long for a young strolling actor who stole her heart while she was at boarding school. Jerry hopes to meet up with this actor and to fight a duel with him, as he believes that he has been wronged by him. The story is complicated: its richness and complexity lies in its telling, which is by means of a series of letters from the various travellers. This epistolary form works to enrich the imaginative texture - not only does it provide the readers with a multi-dimensional view of the characters, situations and events of the narrative, but also — letters being the most intimate possible of written human communications, as Richardson had shown earlier, — it furthers the illusion of the novel's truth to nature. In this way the epistolary novel contributed towards the modernist "stream-of-consciousness".

They stay at Hotwells, Clifton, Bristol, on the way to Bath, and here, unbeknown to themselves, the party re-encounter the young actor, Wilson. He is disguised as a Jewish spectacle-seller and though he makes himself known to the doting Lydia, he escapes detection by the others. Lydia asks Win Jenkins to follow him and find his true identity. Win forgets the name he tells her, but remembers to tell Lydia on her return that he said he was a true gentleman "in which character he would very soon avow his passion.....without fear of censure or reproach...."

The family arrive at Bath, and Tabitha begins her determined search for a marital partner, Matthew savours the waters, and the young people marvel at the splendour and entertainment of the celebrated spa city. They then set off for London. On the way through Wiltshire there is an incident in which Tabitha's lapdog, Chowder, is upset and bites Matthew Bramble's servant. John Thomas, the servant, insists the dog be put to death and loses his temper in the ensuing argument. He is dismissed, together with the postilion. To replace the loss of these menials, Matthew hires Humphry Clinker, a "beggarly rascal" without a shirt to his back:

> ...about twenty years of age, of a middling size, with bandy legs, flat nose, and long chin — but his complexion was of a sickly yellow; his looks denoted famine, and the rags that he wore could hardly conceal what decency requires to be covered....

His story, as related to Matthew Bramble by the landlord of the inn at Marlborough, is a doleful one:

> ...he had been a love begotten babe, brought up in the work-house, and put out apprentice by the parish to a country black-smith, who had died before the boy's time was out: he had for some time worked under his ostler, as a helper and extra postilion, till he was taken ill of the ague, which disabled him from getting his bread: that, having sold or pawned every thing he had in the world for his cure and subsistence, he became so miserable and shabby, that he disgraced the stable, and was dismissed....

Matthew is moved to pity by this sorrowful saga, gives the boy some money to buy decent clothes, and takes him into his employment.

The group continue their journey to London, where Humphry is falsely imprisoned but is eventually cleared and released. They visit Vauxhall Gardens and then leave for Scotland. En route they enjoy adventures at Scarborough, including a scene where Humphry, mistakenly assuming that Bramble was drowning, hauls him naked from the sea, to the great amusement of the onlookers. At Durham, Tabitha meets a gaunt old Scots soldier, Lieutenant Obediah Lismahago, and begins to fall in love with him. Win Jenkins is amorously enchanted by Humphry. The party is lavishly entertained at Edinburgh; Lydia catches sight of Wilson, her young "actor" again. The coach is overturned during the return journey to England and Humphry saves Bramble's life. While recuperating at the local inn, Bramble meets an old college friend, Dennison. In a dénouement that this time, really works, it is disclosed that Humphry is Matthew Bramble's illegitimate son. Lydia's beloved, Wilson, it is revealed, is Dennison's son, George, who had run away from home and become a strolling player in order to escape an arranged marriage. The novel ends with three marriages: Lydia and George, Tabitha and Obediah, Winifred and Humphry. Squire Bramble returns to Brambleton Hall well stocked with good health, to spend the remainder of his days in active country pastimes, especially taking to the heath with his fowling-piece in all weathers.

The plot of *Humphry Clinker* is a deft reworking of several well used novel-conventions and 18th century clichés. Its literary interest and warmth of heart arise from the skill with which Smollett exploits the epistolary technique. Each of the letters reveals the character of its writer. These varying viewpoints work collectively to bring before the reader a rich, dazzling and convincing multi-dimensional view of life in late Hanoverian Britain. Smollett's immortality is guaranteed by the famous set pieces — such as the scenes in Bath and Scotland. But the constant theme of the book is the kind of human injustice that arises from false perceptions and ideological distortions. Smollett is concerned in this novel with how *homo sapiens*, that strange mixture of passion and reason, is self-deceiving in the belief that human actions are rational. He has Jerry Melford enunciate this theme at the end of the book:

> I am ... mortified to reflect what flagrant injustice we every day commit, and what absurd judgement we form, in viewing objects through the falsifying mediums of prejudice and passion.....Without all doubt, the greatest advantage acquired in travelling and perusing mankind in the original, is that of dispelling those shameful clouds that darken the faculties of the mind, preventing it from judging with candour and precision. (14 October).

The first major set-piece in the novel is the sequence in Bath, a city Smollett knew well. He had attempted to earn his living here professionally as a physician in the early 1750's and had visited the spa city for the sake of his own health in 1766. Through Matthew Bramble's eyes we are shown how Bath has declined from its heyday as a centre of fashion as a consequence of the modern craze for luxury and extravagance, the result of ransacking the colonies and scraping huge fortunes together from tobacco and sugar in America and the West Indies, and from plundering the East Indies.

Bath had gone through several socio-economic transformations. From being a centre of the West Country wool trade and an important ecclesiastical city, it was transformed into one of earliest spas after the visit of Anne of Denmark, wife of James I, in 1616. It earned the seal of royal approval from its entertainment of Charles II and his court in 1663. Under Beau Nash, its brilliant Master of Ceremonies, Bath, became the most fashionable spa in the kingdom. Its first Pump Room was built in 1706. It had eight thousand visitors in 1715. Bath offered good medical treatment, spa facilities, brilliant entertainment and social life during the season. This was the city as Smollett knew as a young doctor.

By the time Matthew Bramble arrived at the spa, war, conquest, commerce, trade and colonial and imperial expansion had made Britain a prosperous nation. Those who made money flocked to Bath to flaunt it. But Bath's meridian as a fashionable, elegant spa had passed. It was now the place for successful fortune-hunters, slave-traders, cotton and silk barons, nabobs, sugar merchants, plantation owners and their managers, to flood the city with their ostentation and vulgarity. Times had changed. Matthew writes to Dr Lewis on 5 May 1770:

> About a dozen years ago, many decent families, restricted to small fortunes, besides those that came hither on the score of health, were tempted to settle at Bath, where they could then live comfortably, and even make a genteel appearance, at a small expense: but the madness of the times has made the place too hot for them, and they are now obliged to think of other migrations — some have already fled to the mountains of Wales, and others have retired to Exeter. Thither, no doubt, they will be followed by the flood of luxury and extravagance, which will drive them from place to place to the very Land's End; and there, I suppose, they will be obliged to ship themselves to some other country. Bath is become a mere sink of profligacy and extortion.....

Smollett is describing Bath at a particular moment of its (and its nation's) history. He is portraying the leading spa of the nation reacting as Britain changed from a country which supported itself from its own indigenous resources into a nation which fed its population and provided its luxuries by trading overseas, very largely from its colonies. The city Smollett remembered from the mid-century had changed utterly. As Bramble writes;

....nothing but disappointment at Bath; which is so altered, that I can scarce believe it is the same place that I frequented about thirty years ago ... this place, which Nature and Providence seem to have intended as a resource from distemper and disquiet, is become the very centre of racket and dissipation.....

What is particularly noticeable in the sections on Bath is the sense of social collapse and disintegration of decent values, but carried on a rising tide of luxury. Social display and conspicuous consumption have become the dominant social preoccupations. Human compassion, collectivity, tolerance — qualities such as Bramble shows when he learns of the plight of the unfortunate Humphry (long before he realises he is his son) — no longer count. Bramble's view of Bath is the one which strikes the reader's mind the most forcefully, however charming and exciting the younger ones find it. Lydia writes on 26 April:

Bath is to me a new world. All is gaiety, good humour and diversion. The eye is continually entertained with the splendour of dress and equipage, and the ear with the sound of coaches..... The Squares, the Circus, and the Parades put you in mind of the sumptuous palaces, represented in prints and pictures, and the new buildings ... look like so many enchanted castles, raised on hanging terraces....

These gushing impressions are erased when we read Bramble's words:

Every upstart of fortune, harnessed in the trappings of the mode, present himself at Bath, as in the very focus of observation. Clerks and factors from the East Indies, loaded with the spoil of plundered provinces; planters, negro-drivers and hucksters from our American plantations, enriched they know not how; agents, commissionaries and contractors, who have fattened in two successive wars....usurers, brokers and jobbers of every kind... Knowing no other criterion of greatness, but the ostentation of wealth....all of them hurry to Bath. (23 April)

Smollett, his mind furnished with imagery from his days as a physician and surgeon, presents the decadence of society at Bath in terms of physical morbidity and broken or deformed limbs. Matthew

Bramble faints at the smell at the Assembly Rooms:

> It was indeed a compound of villainous smells.... Imagine to yourself a high exalted essence of mingled odours arising from putrid gums, imposthumated lungs, sour flatulences, rank armpits, seating feet, running sores ... plaster, ointments and embrocations....

Bath has become, he writes "the very racket and centre of dissipation" inhabited by "lunatics". The emphasis is on dirt and disease: "...we know not what sores may be running into the water while we are bathing, and what sort of matter we may thus imbibe; the king's evil, the scurvy, the cancer, and the pox...." No reader will readily forget Bramble's words about "scrophulous ulcers" and "sweat and dirt and dandruff, and the abominable discharges of various kinds, from twenty different bodies" and the orthopedic comparison of the structure and anatomy of the city to his "the wreck of streets and squares disjointed by an earthquake...."

Smollett had worked as doctor at Bath, and had written a learned treatise on the use of the mineral waters there, so his knowledge of the location and expertise is hardly open to question. What he does here is to present the social corruption of the time in terms of a civilisation in a state of physical decay, exhibited in pathological terms.

The Scottish scenes in *Humphry Clinker* also make a very deep and vivid impression on readers. Here, in what was to be his last novel, Smollett seems to repay the compliment he had paid in *Roderick Random*, his first novel. In 1748 we had the views of young Scot, Roderick, on his adventures in English society. In these Scottish episodes — about fifty pages — Smollett offers a rich and varied portrait of several aspects of Scottish life at a particular stage in his nation's development. Smollett loved Scotland: recollecting it always warmed his heart, which was not untainted by bitterness.

Smollett's case is that the basis of the conflict between Scotland and England is ignorance. As Jerry Melford writes on 18 July from Haddington: "....South Britons in general are woefully ignorant..... What, between want of curiosity, and traditional sarcasms, the effect of ancient animosity, the people at the other end of the island know as little of Scotland as of Japan". Using the persona of Matthew Bramble, writing from Edinburgh, Smollett argues that much of the distortion of Scotland's reputation by the English is the result of prejudice, resulting from the artificial maintenance of its "provincial" nature. Consequently, the English always "compare" Scottish institutions, life and culture with England. The false sense of difference invites unfavourable comparison, whereas we should regard Scotland and England as aspects of the same nation:

> The first impressions which an Englishman receives in this country, will not contribute to the removal of his prejudices; became he refers everything he sees to a comparison with the same articles in his own country; and this comparison is unfavourable to Scotland in all its exteriors, such as the face of the country in respect to cultivation, the appearance of the bulk of the people, and the language of conversation in general....I think the Scots would do well, for their own sakes, to adopt the English idioms and pronunciation; for those of them especially, who are resolved to push their fortunes in South-Britain — I know, by experience, how easily an Englishman is influenced by the ear, and how apt he is to laugh, when he hears his own language spoken with a foreign or provincial accent.....(Matthew Bramble, letter 8 August)

Bramble goes to great lengths to stress the generosity, hospitality and kindness which they meet wherever they go. He praises their legal system, local government and the high standard of academic scholarship. The architectural sights delight him. Edinburgh, he says, is a "hot-bed of genius" where he makes the acquaintance of "many authors of the first distinction". This was the age of the Scottish Enlightenment, of David Hume, the philosopher and historian, who was the centre of Edinburgh's intellectual and literary life; John Home, private secretary to the Earl of Bute (author of the celebrated tragedy, *Douglas* 1757, at the first night of which an anonymous voice called out "whaur's yer Wully Shakespeare noo?"); William Robertson, the historian (author of *History of Scotland* 1759, *History of the Reign of the Emperor Charles V* 1769); Adam Smith, the political economist; Robert Wallace, the writer on population; Revd. Hugh Blair, Regius

Professor of Rhetoric and Belles-Lettres at Edinburgh (his *Sermons,* five volumes 1777-1800 were to become celebrated); Adam Ferguson, Professor of Philosophy at Edinburgh and William Wilkie, the "Scottish Homer" (his *The Epigoniad* 1757, in heroic couplets, was a version of the fourth book of the *Iliad*). Bramble actually meets and converses with these sages, through his intermediary Dr Alexander Carlyle, minister of Inveresk, Midlothian, who was, in fact, a very good friend of Smollett's, and wrote much about him in his *Autobiography.*

The accounts of the landscape are colourful and vivid. The Brambles stay with James Smollett, the cousin, (whose heir-presumptive Tobias was).

> From Dumbarton, the West Highlands appear in the form of huge, dusky mountains, piled one over another....We have fixed our headquarters at Cameron, a very neat country-house belonging to commissary Smollett, where we found every sort of accommodation we could desire — It is situated like a Druid's temple, in a grove of oak, close by the side of Lough-Lomond, which is a surprising body of pure transparent water, unfathomably deep in many places, six or seven miles broad, four and twenty miles in length, displaying above twenty green islands, covered with wood; some of them cultivated for corn, and many of them stocked with red deer — They belong to different gentlemen, whose seats are scattered along the banks of the lake, which are agreeably romantic beyond all conception.....This country appears more and more wild and savage the further we advance; and the people are as different from the Low-land Scots, in their looks, garb, and language, as the mountaineers of Brecknock are from the inhabitants of Hertfordshire. (Jerry Melford 3 September)

These cultural differences, Jerry records, exhibit themselves at all levels. Lowlanders drink weak table-beer when they socialise. Highlanders quaff whisky from their cradles. Highlanders eat more animal food — deer, game, sheep. The peasants, he observed, live at a very wretched level, in cabins. Poor Highlanders suffer the most, disarmed by Act of Parliament, deprived of the "ancient garb", compelled to wear breeches and debarred from wearing Tartan "which was their own manufacture, prized by them above all the velvets, brocades and tissues of Europe and Asia". The government, he writes, "could not have taken a more effectual method to break their national spirit". It is Jerry who is particularly alert to the latent romantic spirit of the locality:

> We have had princely sport in hunting the stag on these mountains — These are the lonely hills of Morven, where Fingal and his heroes enjoyed the same pastime; I feel an enthusiastic pleasure when I survey the brown heath that Ossian wont to tread; and hear the wind whistle through the bending grass — when I enter our landlord's hall, I look for the suspended harp of that divine bard, and listen in hopes of hearing the aerial sound of his respected spirit.....(ibid)

The much lauded scenes of Highland domestic hospitality in Walter Scott's *Waverley*, often cited in discussions about the awakening dawn of Romanticism, are prefigured in this section of *Humphry Clinker*. Had these pages of Smollett's work been better known, the sources of Scott's construction of the historical imagination would have been more fully revealed.

Matthew Bramble detects the sublime at James Smollett's seat at Cameron:

> ....so embosomed in an oak wood, that we did not see it till we were within fifty yards of the door. I have seen the Lago di Garda, Albano, De Vico, Bolsena and Geneva, and, upon my honour, I prefer Lough-Lomond to them all, a preference which is certainly owing to the verdant islands that seem to float upon its surface, affording the most enchanting objects of repose to the excursive view. Nor are the banks destitute of beauties, which even partake of the sublime. On this side they display a sweet variety of woodland, cornfield, and pasture, with several agreeable villas emerging as it were out of the lake, till, at some distance, the prospect terminates in huge mountains covered with heath, which being in the bloom, affords a very rich covering of purple. Every thing here is romantic beyond imagination. This country is stiled the Arcadia of Scotland.... What say you to a natural bason of pure water, near thirty miles long, and in some places seven miles broad, and in many above a hundred fathoms deep, having four and twenty habitable islands, some of them stocked with deer, and all of them covered with wood; containing immense quantities of delicious fish....and finally communicating with the sea, by sending off the Leven....(28 August)

Bramble then quotes a poem, *Ode to Leven Water*, explaining that these these lines were written "by Dr Smollett, who was born on the banks of it, within two miles of the place where I am now writing....." This poem, which was first published in *Town and Country Magazine* in June 1771, is, not of the first rank:

> On Leven's banks, while free to rove,
> And tune the rural pipe to love;
> I envied not the happiest swain
> That ever trod th' Arcadian plain.
> Pure stream! in whose transparent wave
> My youthful limbs I wont to lave;

but it shows Smollett's love of Scotland.

The series of marriages and reunions with which the novel concludes carries, as did those marriages in the last Act of so many Elizabethan and Jacobean comedies, a sense of human warmth and reconciliation. Smollett's bitter satiric vein has become subdued. Near to death, at the end of an astonishingly active and creative literary career, Smollett seems to shake hands with humanity as — many miles from Scotland — he finally returns in imagination to the rhapsodically beautiful land which gave him birth.

Smollett's three best novels — *Roderick Random, Peregrine Pickle* and *Humphry Clinker* — are classics. Nevertheless, in several quite fundamental respects — creation of character, plot construction, satiric and moral intention — they are also a now well-acknowledged part of the beginning of the English novel as a significant modern literary genre. It is a mistake to preserve Smollett's fiction in the aspic of "the 18th century novel". On the face of it, it seems vigorously to grow naturally from the soil of the 18th century. Nevertheless it is undeniable that the roots of that great tree whose fruit the Victorians were so lavishly to harvest in the works of Dickens and George Eliot are clearly discernible in the novels of Smollett, as well as those of his contemporaries, Richardson and Fielding.

V CRITICAL OVERVIEW: SMOLLETT TODAY

Although Smollett died well over two hundred years ago, created several masterpieces in various genres, was an inspiration to several subsequent novelists who imitated him much to their own advancement and benefit, is still in print, sells and is quitey widely read — he has not yet achieved that final accolade which renders him a true British classic. As David Daiches argues, Smollett continues to something of an odd man out in our literature: "he has not come in for modern revaluation as one of the pioneers of the English novel, as have Defoe, Richardson and Fielding". He is not discussed, except for an occasional casual aside, in Ian Watt's influential study, *The Rise of the English Novel*: indeed, Watt specifically excludes Smollett, observing that he "has many merits as a social reporter and as a humourist, but the manifest flaws in the central situations and the general structure of all his novels except *Humphry Clinker* .... prevent him from playing a very important role in the main tradition of the novel. 'He is wholly excluded from F.R.Leavis's 'great tradition' of English fiction".

Smollett's novels received much notice when they were first published. He was engaged in literary controversy with Richardson and Fielding and as the founder and editor of a literary critical journal of considerable influence (and historic importance) — *The Critical Review* — but his official reputation as a leading man of letters and novelist went into decline soon after his death. His work continued to be widely read, and, admired by writers and novelists, his reputation was kept alive almost in an 'underground' fashion. By contrast, Fielding's reputation - despite Dr. Johnson's famous disapproval - grew.

Smollett has yet to be awarded *academic* recognition in Britain. There is a surprisingly limited amount of critical attention devoted to him. Although he has had sturdy supporters in universities overseas, notably in America and France, (G.S.Rousseau at the University of California at Los Angeles and Paul-Gabriel Bouce at the Sorbonne), he has yet to be granted recognition by the so-called leaders of literary opinion in British Universities.

Recognition from Dr Johnson

Tobias Smollett was respected for his learning by his contemporaries; indeed, he was mocked for it by a few. Dr Johnson was sure that Smollett would continue to be read by future generations of the sophisticated and the learned. As Smollett is so frequently accused in modern times of crudity of style and coarseness of humour, it is worth looking carefully at the evidence for this. Some is to be found in James Boswell's *A Journal of a Tour to the Hebrides* (1785). The travellers are taken to Cameron where they meet James Smollett, the novelist's cousin, "a man of considerable learning", Boswell records, "with abundance of animal spirits, so that he was a very good companion for Dr Johnson". In order to commemorate his distinguished cousin, the novelist, James Smollett tells Dr Johnson that he had erected a pillar on the high road to Glasgow. He and sought Dr Johnson's advice as to an inscription for it:

> Lord Kames, who, though he had a great store of knowledge, with much ingenuity, and uncommon activity of mind, was no profound scholar, had it seems recommended an English inscription. Dr Johnson treated this with great contempt, saying, 'An English inscription would be a disgrace to Dr Smollett'; and, in answer to what Lord Kames had urged, as to the advantage of its being in English, because it would be generally understood, I observed, that all to whom Dr Smollett's merit could be an object of respect and imitation, would understand it as well in Latin; and that surely it was not meant for Highland drovers, or other such people, who pass and repass that way.
> We were then shown a Latin inscription, proposed for this monument. Dr Johnson sat down with an ardent and liberal earnestness to revise it, and greatly improved it by several additions and variations.....

Dr Johnson, then, revised the Latin inscription and added much by way of effusive praise of Scotland's great novelist. Despite this Smollett has achieved little reputation amongst British scholars and academics, who prefer to exercise their active intellects wrestling with the various manifestations of "Modernism". But there has always been an "underground" Smollett industry among good journalists, novelists such as Dickens and literary practitioners. Working writers as distinct from "leaders of literary opinion" have always taken Smollett to their hearts, and welcomed him as a fellow professional. To his contemporaries he seemed a man of multifarious talents and abilities — a prolific journalist and editor, a formidable historian, satirist, poet, writer for the stage and a man of science. That he was additionally a brilliantly successful and popular novelist must have made people think that the Scottish tag "a man o' parts" was indeed designed specifically with Tobias George Smollett in mind. Johnson (again) wrote an essay in *The Rambler* on 31 March 1750, after the publication of *Roderick Random* and *Tom Jones*, in which he welcomed these works, and discussed the novelty of such narrative prose fiction Smollett was then in the process of pioneering. He clearly perceived that what was here in the making was a new contribution to literature, a new departure in creative writing. The creation of the novel in Britain at this time was in part brought about by the restrictions affecting writing for the stage — writing for the theatre had traditionally offered considerable rewards to aspiring authors — as much as by developments in printing and publishing which caused the book trade to flourish. The theatre was restricted as a result of Robert Walpole's Licensing Act of 1737, which required all productions to be approved by the Lord Chancellor. This in effect put an end to Fielding's career as a dramatist, and severely limited opportunities which had previously encouraged writers. Johnson wrote:

> The works of fiction, with which the present generation seems more particularly delighted, are such as exhibit life in its true state, diversified only by accidents that daily happen in the world, and influenced by passions and qualities which are really to be found in conversing with mankind.
>
> This kind of writing may be termed not improperly the comedy of romance, and is to be conducted nearly by the rules of comic poetry. Its province is to bring about natural events by easy means, and to keep up curiosity without the help of

wonder: it is therefore precluded from the machines and expedients of the heroic romance....

Smollett Praised by the Romantic Essayists

Johnson notes that these new novels are true to contemporary life, that they entertain by an imitation of life, and while they do warrent the classification of "romance" — they are free from the traditional machinery of romances — magic, enchantment, giants, fairies and all the rest of the apparatus. Oliver Goldsmith admired Smollett, and attested his admiration several times. Robert Burns praised Smollett's "incomparable humour". William Godwin, writing in *The Enquirer: Reflections on Education, Manners, and Literature* (1797), commented on Smollett's genius and peculiar excellence, while reserving judgement on his style, which Godwin found lacking in adornment and polish:

> In all his works of invention, we find the stamp of a mighty mind. In his lightest sketches, there is nothing frivolous, trifling and effeminate. In his most glowing portraits, we acknowledge a mind at ease, rather essaying its powers, than tasking them. We applaud his works....

Smollett's ability to tell a story, to place believable characters before the reader, to engage sympathy, to amuse, instruct and move the readers without seeming to come at him with palpable intent, was admired by Charles Lamb, who wrote to Wordsworth in 1801:

> An intelligent reader finds a sort of insult in being told, I will teach you how to think upon this subject. This fault, if I am right, is in a ten-thousandth worse degree to be found in Sterne and many other novelists & modern poets, who continually put a sign post up to shew where you are to feel. They set out with assuming their readers to be stupid. Very different from Robinson Crusoe, the Vicar of Wakefield, Roderick Random, and other beautiful bare narratives.

Leigh Hunt, who strongly objected to qualities he found "disgusting" in Smollett, readily admitted his comicality, and interestingly qualified the claims of his tendency to corrupt readers:

> Though Smollett sometimes vexes us with the malicious boy's-play of his heroes, and sometimes disgusts us with his coarseness, he is still the Smollett whom now, as in one's boyhood, it is impossible not to heartily laugh with. He is accomplished writer, and a masterly observer, and may be called the finest of caricaturits. His caricatures are always substantially true: it is only the complexional vehemence of his gusto that leads him to toss them up as he does, and tumble them on to our plates. Then as to the objections against his morality, nobody will be hurt by it. The delicate and sentimental will look on the whole matter as a joke; the accessories of the characters will deter them: while readers of a coarser taste, for whom their friends might fear most because they are most likely to be conversant with the senes described, are, in our opinion, to be seriously benefitted by the perusal; for it will show them, that heroes of their description are expected to have virtues as well as faults, and that they seldom get anything by being positively disagreeable or bad. Our author's lovers, it must be owned are not of the most sentimental or flattering description. One of their commonest modes of paying their court, even to those they best love and esteem, is by writing lampoons on other women! Smollett had a strong spice of pride and malice in him (greatly owing, we doubt not, to some scene of unjust treatment he witnessed in early youth), which he imparts to his heroes; all of whom, probably, are caricatures of himself, as Fielding's brawny, good-natured, idle fellows are of him. There is no serious evil intention, however. It is all out of resentment of some evil, real or imaginary, or is made up of pure animal spirit and the love of venting a complexional sense of power. It is energy, humour, and movement, not particularly amiable, but clever, entertaining, and interesting, and without an atom of hypocrisy in it. No man will learn to be shabby by reading Smollett's writings. (Leigh Hunt: Table Talk, 1851)

Nor, of course should we miss Smollett's own ironic depreciation of any "tendency to corrupt".

Hazlitt's Views

William Hazlitt's published opinions on Smollett are a curious mixture. They appeared originally in *The Edinburgh Magazine* in 1814 (Volume XXIV) and were later published in *Lectures on the English Comic Writers* (1819). He asserts that *Roderick Random* is his finest novel, and claims that it has "a much more modern air" than *Tom Jones,* which was published about the same time. This is the result, Hazlitt believes, of Smollett's being a young man at the time, whereas Fielding's "manner must have been formed long before". He finds the style of this novel more scholarly and pointed, and containing more rapid action, even at the cost of reading rather like "detached anecdotes taken from a newspaper". Hazlitt, though ready to praise the brilliant and "realistic" surface quality of Smollett's fiction complains that, unlike Fielding, he does not see beneath the surface, he seldom:

> ...probes to the quick, or penetrates beyond the surface of his characters, and therefore leaves no stings in the minds of his readers, and in this manner is far less interesting than Fielding. His novels always enliven, and never tire us: we take them up with pleasure, and lay them down without any strong feeling of regret. We look on and laugh, as spectators of an amusing though inelegant scene, without closing in on with the combatants, or being made parties of the event....

Smollett, in Hazlitt's view, is a caricaturist, but Fielding was a painter. He argues this distinction at some length, dismisses *Pickle* as being no great favourite of his and says that *Launcelot Greaves* was not worthy of Smollett's genius. He then concludes with the claim that *Humphry Clinker* and *Count Fathom* "are both equally admirable in their way". This is a startling statement which his following discussion does little to support, though it contains the celebrated comment (oft quoted in blurbs for this novel) that Clinker is "the most pleasant gossiping novel that ever was written". Hazlitt has little useful whatsoever to say about the extraordinary construction of this masterpiece. In place of any serious analysis the reader is merely offered a few lines of generally approving comment about Smollett's masterly creation of the characters — Win, Humphry, Tabitha and the rest of them. He gives the palm to Lismahago — "the best preserved, and most original of all Smollett's characters". Smollett's Lismahago is, according to Hazlitt, the Scotsman's Scotsman. He develops this view in an essay on

'On the Scotch Character' published in *The Liberal*, in January 1823. Hazlitt's comments are a matter of considerable critical interest since he makes such a point of praising Smollett's genius in putting before the readers of fiction characters whose reality we accept as thoroughly convincing.

Fellow Scot, Thomas Carlyle: Comedy and Pathos

Thomas Carlyle could find no words too extravagant to laud his fellow Scot. As a writer, Smollett was incomparable. Carlyle's praise seems almost outlandish. He claims that Smollett excels Dante. However, despite this characteristic misuse of hyperbole, Carlyle does superbly locate the powerful combination of the comic and the pathetic which is so typical (and so neglected) a feature of Smollett's art:

> I remember few happier days than those in which I ran off into the fields to read Roderick Random, and how inconsolable I was that I could not get the second volume.To this day I know of few writers equal to Smollett. Humphry Clinker is precious to me now as he was in those years. Nothing by Dante or anyone else surpasses in pathos the scene where Humphry goes into the smithy made for him in the old house, and whilst he is heating the iron, the poor woman who has lost her husband, and is deranged, comes and talks to him as to her husband. 'John, they told me you were dead. How glad I am you have come!' And Humphry's tears fall down and bubble on the hot iron.

Maturin

Although neglected today, the good opinion of fellow novelist and dramatist Charles Robert Maturin (1782-1824), now rightly back in the centre of attention for his *Melmoth*, is relevant. Maturin was curate of St Peter's, Dublin and was for a time a school headmaster before turning successfully to literature. His tragedy *Bertram*, recommended by Scott and Byron, was staged with great success at Drury Lane by Kean in 1816. In a review of Maria Edgeworth's *Harrington and Ormond, Tales* (1817) published in *The British Review and London*

Critical Journal in 1818, Maturin discussed Smollett's qualities as a novelist. He singled out Smollett's extremely varied knowledge of the human character, his extensive experience of life in all its ups and downs, and stressed that he was a man of parts, wide ranging skills. He rightly asserted that in the main his leading figures — Roderick, Pickle and the rest of them — are all more or less drawn on himself and consequently much the same. Bramble, he interestingly claims, is really an elderly version of this same character. They are all:

> ... portraits of the same character in various costumes. The same Quixotic gallantry in love and courage, the same high sentiment of honour struggling with depravity of habit and virulence of temper, the same morbid and morose sensibility, the same supercilious courtesy, and misanthropic benevolence. Smollett is said to have sat to himself for the portrait of his own heroes; if so, Smollett with all the advantages of talent, experience, and spirit was as unhappy as he was unamiable.

By this time, social mores having changed, Maturin knew that he was obliged to comment on Smollett's alleged coarseness. What seemed, to readers of Jane Austen's generation indelicate in Smollett's fiction, Maturin asserted, was the honesty of Smollett's portrait of life. Unlike Fielding, Smollett did not seek out impure scenes "with insatiable, fulsome, gloating avidity" — Smollett's humour seems coarse to modern readers because taste has changed, and further, the nature of his subjects sometimes required Smollett to paint life in all its varieties, however indelicate: "It may be said 'impurity lay in his way, and he found it'..."

Coleridge: Smollett's Humours

In the same year that Maturin's article was published, Samuel Taylor Coleridge delivered a lecture at the Philosophical Society, Fetter Lane, London, on 24 February. In speaking on 'Wit and Humour', he found "exquisite humour" in Strap, Lieutenant Bowling and Morgan (in *Roderick Random*) and in Matthew Bramble

(*Humphry Clinker*) "while in his Peregrine Pickle we find an abundance of drollery, which too often degenerates into mere oddity" Coleridge was inclined to associate this with the Elizabethan psychology and the Four Humours (Melancholy, Choleric, Phlegmatic and Sanguine) as exploited by Ben Jonson.

A person whose humours were equally balanced would be sanguine, they would be ruddy of complexion, fair and optimistic. The choleric person is yellow, thin, bad-tempered and rash. The phlegmatic person is fat, dull and slow-witted. The melancholic is dark, lean and anxious. In effect, these are almost mechanical explanations of character. Coleridge was the first to discern that many of the characters in Smollett's fiction were constructed on similar principles, and of course the tradition so skilfully used by Ben Jonson in his "humours" plays and elsewhere, is customarily traced through to Dickens. There is little "psychological" explanation of people's behaviour. They act as they do, because they are what they are. In this not necessarily unsubtle view of human character, people are the victims of what could be called their essences. This, Coleridge believed, helped to explain:

> ....the congeniality of humour with pathos, so exquisite in Sterne and Smollett, and hence also the tender feeling which we always have for, and associate with, the humours or hobby-horses of a man. First, we respect a humourist, because absence of interested motive is the ground-work of the character, although the imagination of an interest may exist in the individual himself, as if a remarkably simple-hearted man should pride himself on his knowledge of the world, and how ell he can manage it: — and secondly, there always is in a genuine humour an acknowledgement of the hollowness and farce of the world, and its disproportion to the godlike within us. (Lecture IX of the 1818 series of Lectures)

This comment touches on two very important aspects of Smollett's art as one of the great humorous writers. Coleridge acknowledges Smollett's genius in creating comic situations, plots, incidents, sequences; but he also locates him in an ancient and worthy tradition of character creation which goes right back to Theophrastus, (circa 370-286 BC) author of *Characters*, who pioneered character creation;

through the Commedia dell Arte (15th-16th century), which was based on the comic interaction between character types; and was exploited by Shakespeare and Ben Jonson especially in *Love's Labours Lost* (1594) and *Every Man in his Humour* (1598) respectively. Coleridge thus identified Smollett as drawing upon, and contributing to, an ancient and honourable literary tradition.

Championed by Sir Walter Scott

Two of Smollett's greatest champions were the leading literary giants of the first half of the 19th century — Sir Walter Scott and Charles Dickens. Scott first read Smollett's novels when he was a pupil at Kelso Grammar School, borrowing them, along with Richardson's, Fielding's and Henry Mackenzie's *The Man of Feeling*, from Kelso's circulating library. Later in life, in a letter to his publisher James Ballantyne, Scott asserted that for him Fielding and Smollett were "the fathers of the novel". In his declining months the author of the *Waverley Novels* personally identified himself with Smollett and feared — like his great fellow countryman — that he would be driven abroad by ill health and leave his bones in a foreign country.

In the years 1821-4 James Ballantyne, the Edinburgh printer and publisher, who had been at school with Scott, published *Ballantyne's Novelists' Library*, and Scott was commissioned to write the *Lives of the Novelists*, as prefaces to the various novelists' works. Scott commented usefully on Smollett's work, praising his truth to life, his comicality and his use of real-life characters as originals. He had some interesting things to say about Smollett's influences (especially Le Sage) and pioneering of the novel form by developing the romance so that it could accommodate a view of modern life. He drew attention, too, to the essentially satiric basis of much of Smollett's fiction. When he comes to discuss the various merits of Fielding and Smollett the author of the Waverley Novels has much insight and value to impart. Both novelists wrote for the stage, both dabbled in politics, both wrote as travellers and both were masters of the new form, the novel, which was to a large extent of their creation. Fielding, Scott believed, had a higher and purer taste, and more elegance of composition and expression:

> ....a nearer approach to the grave irony of Swift and Cervantes; a great deal more address or felicity in the conduct of his story.... a power of describing amiable and virtuous characters, and of placing before us heroes, and especially heroines, of a much higher as well as pleasing character than Smollett was able to present....

The reader nods in agreement with this verdict. But then, Scott surprises us by asserting that Smollett's superiority lies in his rich and inventive genius, in which capacity he finds Fielding limited. Scott locates that seemingly inexhaustible and energetic imagination so characteristic of Smollett, right to the very end. Fielding had shot his bolt with Tom Jones:

> .....If Fielding had superior taste, the palm of more brilliancy of genius, more inexhaustible richness of invention, must in justice be awarded to Smollett. In comparison with his sphere, that in which Fielding walked was limited; and, compared with the wealthy profusion of varied character and incident which Smollett has scattered through his works, there is a poverty of composition about his rival. Fielding's fame rests on a single chef d'oeuvre; and the art and industry which produced Tom Jones, was unable to rise to equal excellence in Amelia. Though, therefore, we may justly prefer Tom Jones as the most masterly example of an artful and well told novel, to any individual work of Smollett; yet, Roderick Random, Peregrine Pickle, and Humphry Clinker, do each of them far excel Joseph Andrews or Amelia; and to descend still lower Jonathan Wild, or The Journey to the Next World, cannot be put into momentary comparison with Sir Launcelot Greaves, or Ferdinand Count Fathom.

Scott then went on to testify to his belief that every successful novelist must be more or less a poet. Smollett was, of course, a poet in the traditional sense — he wrote verse. But Scott does not mean simply verse-writing. He refers to that specially heightened quality in the imagination which a true novelist must have, an especial power of enchantment which he is able to cast over his attempts to capture the realities of life they elect to write about.

The quality of imagination is absolutely indispensable to him: his accurate power of examining and embodying human character and human passion, as well as the external face of nature, is not less essential; and the talent of describing well what he feels with acuteness, added to the above requisites, goes far to complete the poetic character. Smollett was, even in the ordinary sense, which limits the name to those who write verses, a poet of distinction; and, in this particular, superior to Fielding, who seldom aims at more than a slight translation from the classics. Accordingly, if he is surpassed by Fielding in moving pity, the northern novelist soars far above him in his powers of exciting terror. Fielding has no passages which approach in sublimity to the robber scene in Count Fathom; or to the terrible description of a sea-engagement, in which Roderick Random sits chained and exposed upon the poop, without the power of motion or exertion, during the carnage of a tremendous engagement. Smollett's descriptions ascend to the sublime; and, in general, there is an air of romance in his writings, which raise his narratives above the level and easy course of ordinary life. He was .... a searcher of dark bosoms, and loved to paint characters under the strong agitation of fierce and stormy passions. Hence, misanthropes, gamblers, and duellists are as common in his works as robbers in in those of Salvator Rosa, and are drawn, in most cases, with the same terrible truth and effect......

Scott compares like with like. He compares Smollett's portrayal of the genuinely villainous Count Fathom with the abstract villainy of Fielding's Jonathan Wild. Fathom, he argues, is a truly terrifying human portrait whereas Fielding's villain is a tiresome, mechanical bore. Scott praises Smollett's profuse fancy, and the unlaboured manner in which his invention piles incident upon incident and character upon character. He admires the manner in which he refuses, for the most part, to interpose his personality between the reader and the action of the narrative ("He manages his delightful puppet-show without thrusting his head beyond the curtain...to explain what he is doing...") and is particularly generous in the commendation of Smollett's portrayal of sea characters, stressing the manner in which Smollett carefully delineates individual characters within the accurate, convincing and well-observed context of professional naval life and war service. He awards Fielding the palm when it comes to grave irony in the manner of Cervantes, but relishes Smollett's robust good humour, comicality and keen eye for the ludicrous in real life. His summing up is magisterial:

> Upon the whole, the genius of Smollett may be said to resemble that of Rubens. His pictures are often deficient in grace; sometimes coarse, and even vulgar in conception; deficient too in keeping, and in due subordination of parts to each other, and intimating too much carelessness on the part of the artist. But these faults are redeemed by such richness and brilliancy of colours; such a profusion of imagination — now bodying forth the grand and the terrible — now the natural, the easy, and the ludicrous; there is so much of life, action, and bustle, in every group he has painted, so much force and individuality of character, that we readily grant to Smollett an equal rank with his great rival Fielding, while we place both far above any of their successors in the same line of fictitious composition.

Charles Dickens: An Expert Witness

We could not wish for a more convincing and credible expert witness to appear at the bar of literary judgement than Scott, unless it be Charles Dickens. Boz was steeped in English fiction, and particularly well acquainted with the 18th century comic novelists. His "debt" to Smollett is easily and frequently referred to, but in fact it needs serious qualification. When *Pickwick Papers* first appeared readers noted qualities in Boz which were reminiscent of Smollett. During its serialisation the journal, *John Bull*, declared that "Smollett never did anything better": the comparison was apt enough in its context. If the influence were not sufficiently testified in the evidence of Dickens's fictions, then we have the remarkable statement he made to his close friend, John Forster, in 1847. He promised Forster that he would supply him with some autobiographical details which he might use for his biography. Dickens built up from early childhood a thorough grounding in the English classics. His father had a small collection of books stored in an upstairs room in the family home:

> From that blessed little room, Roderick Random, Peregrine Pickle, Humphry Clinker, Tom Jones, The Vicar of Wakefield, Don Quixote, Gil Blas and Robinson

70

Crusoe came out, a glorious host, to keep me company. They kept alive my fancy, and my hope of something beyond that place and time — they, and my hope of something beyond that place and time — they, and the Arabian Nights, and the Tales of the Genii — and did me no harm; for, whatever harm there was in some of them, was not there for me; I knew nothing of it. It is astonishing to me now, how I found time, in the midst of my porings and blunderings over heavier themes, to read those books as I did. It is curious to me how I could ever have consoled myself under my small troubles (which were great troubles to me), by impersonating my favourite characters in them.... I have been Tom Jones (a child's Tom Jones, a harmless creature) for a week together. I have sustained my own idea of Roderick Random for a month at a stretch, I verily believe..... When I think of it, the picture always rises in my mind, of a summer evening, the boys at play in the churchyard, and I sitting on my bed reading as if for life. Every barn in the neighbourhood, every stone in the church, and every foot of the churchyard, had some association of its own, in my mind, connected with these books, and stood for some locality made famous in them. I have seen Tom Pipes go climbing up the church steeple; I have watched Strap, with the knapsack on his back, stopping to rest himself upon the wicket-gate; and I know that Commodore Trunnion held that club with Mr Pickle in the parlour of our little village alehouse.....('Autobiographical Fragment', in John Forster: The Life of Charles Dickens, 1872, Book I, Chapter 1)

There is much to note in this passage, but of outstanding significance here is Dickens's complete identification with these novelists' characters to the exclusion of all else. In particular he picks on Smollett. In a letter to the artist Frank Stone, sending him the first volume of Pickle to read, dated 30 May 1854, he says that he believes Smollett's best novel is *Humphry Clinker*, but cannot decide between the varying merits of *Roderick Random* and *Peregrine Pickle*, both of which he admires. These novels are "both extraordinarily good in their way, which is a way without tenderness, but you will have to read them both..." In the seventh chapter of *David Copperfield*, when he is recounting how David, suffering the persecution of the dreaded Mr Murdstone, seeks consolation from immersing himself in reading fiction, he refers again to this obsession with Smollett's novels.

Smollett's influence is also obvious in the famous, much read but critically neglected novels of Captain Frederick Marryatt. Once again we witness a case of a professional writer being kept alive by his readers rather than by academic literary opinion.

The rejection by academics and loyalty of the professional writers continues as a feature of Smollett's reputation in Britain in the 20th century. When we come to examine the process by means of which English Literature was constructed as an academic discipline, acceptable as a part of the university curriculum, we find Smollett and his contemporaries are seldom given the treatment they deserve. Lord David Cecil finds it easy to assert that *Roderick Random* and *Tom Jones* are "constructed on the same lines" (and this is not all — he lumps together *Waverley* and *Nicholas Nickleby* for good measure) and talks about Fielding and Smollett as if they were more or less the same person, or, at least, interchangeable. (*Early Victorian Novelists: Essays in Revaluation* 1935). The Leavises, who were enormously influential in their endeavour to evaluate the achievements of our literature, were overt in their search for moral values. Consequently they inherited an important strain of English puritanism. They tended to confuse earnestness for seriousness and the developed an impressive lack of sympathy with the comedic, except insofar as it could smuggled on board under the guise of irony. The result was that an entire tradition in our literature almost got wiped from the official record — Smollett, Fielding, Goldsmith, Sterne were unceremoniously shown the door, and, until a late change of mind, of Dickens' dazzling output only *Hard Times,* passed muster.

The neglect of Smollett was given the authority of a literary fiat. Despite this proscription, people continued to read 18th century novels. But as always we find that the journeymen and master-craftsmen of the trade valued Smollett's work. Writing in *Tribune* in 1944 George Orwell praised Smollett's "outstanding intellectual honesty" and singled out *Roderick Random* and *Peregrine Pickle* as his masterpieces, and claimed that they contain "some of the best passages of sheer farce in the English language". The qualities Orwell admired in Smollett are his ability to take life whole, to uphold simple, plain virtues and to expose cruelty and the incompetence of those placed in authority over us: "Smollett had been for a while in the navy, and in *Roderick Random* we are given not only an unvarnished account of the Cartagena expedition, but an extraordinarily vivid and disgusting description of the inside of a warship, in those days a sort of floating compendium of disease, discomfort, tyranny and incompetence. The command of Roderick's ship is for a while given to a young man of family, a scented homosexual fop who has hardly seen a ship in his life, and who spends the whole voyage in his cabin to avoid contact with the vulgar sailor-men.... The scenes in the debtors' prison are even better. One of Roderick's fellow prisoners is so reduced that he has no clothes at all and preserves decency as best he can by wearing a very long beard. Some of the prisoners....are poets, and the book contains a self-contained story, 'Mr Melopoyn's Tragedy' which should make anyone who thinks aristocratic patronage a good basis for literature think twice". (George Orwell: 'Tobias Smollett:Scotland's Best Novelist', in *Tribune* 22 September 1944)

The current fashion in English academic criticism has been to flirt - more or less openly - with various forms of structuralism and then deconstructionism. Of course, Smollett could be dealt with in this way, as well as any other writer. Or could he? There is an earthiness about him which resists it. The fact is, he is both in part responsible for a mainstream tradition in British fiction - the tradition that runs from Nashe through him to Marryat, Dickens, Gissing and Orwell himself. It lends itself to overtly "Literary" evaluation, and yet it provides indispensible nourishment for literature.

Smollett resists his critic as eagerly as he awaits him. Energetic, "male" though given to tenderness, acid, bitter, corrosive, essentially decent, his peculiar vividness will survive as long as fiction survives - and will always threaten it when it gets into danger of becoming too attenuated.

SELECT BIBLIOGRAPHY

(a) Works by Smollett

√ *Roderick Random*, edited by Paul Gabriel Bouce (Oxford, World's Classics, Oxford University Press) 1981

Peregrine Pickle, edited by James L. Clifford (Oxford, Oxford University Press) 1983

Ferdinand Count Fathom, edited by Peter Wagner (Harmondsworth, Penguin Books) 1988

Sir Launcelot Greaves, edited by Peter Wagner (Harmondsworth, Penguin Books) 1994

Humphry Clinker, edited by Angus Ross (Harmondsworth, Penguin Books) 1967

Travels Through France and Italy, edited by Frank Felsenstein (Oxford, World's Classics, Oxford University Press) 1981

√ *History and Adventures of an Atom*, edited by Robert Adams Day (University of Georgia Press) 1992

(b) Biography

G.M.Kahrl: *Tobias Smollett, Traveller-Novelist* (Chicago University Press, 1945)

Lewis M. Knapp: *Tobias Smollett: Doctor of Men and Manners* (Princeton, Princeton University Press 1949. Reprinted, New York, Russell and Russell, 1963)

Lewis M. Knapp (editor): *The Letters of Tobias Smollett* (Oxford, Clarendon Press, 1970)

L.L.Martz *The Later Career of Tobias Smollett* (Yale University Press, 1942)

Lewis Melville: *The Life and Letters of Tobias Smollett* (London, Faber and Gwyer, 1926)

(c) Works on Smollett

James G. Basker: *Tobias Smollett: Critic and Journalist* (Newark, Delaware, University of Delaware Press) 1991

Alan Bold (Editor) *Smollett: Author of the First Distinction* (London, Vision Press) 1982

Paul-Gabriel Bouce: *The Novels of Tobias Smollett*, translated by Antonia White (London, Longman,1976)

Donald Bruce: *Radical Doctor Smollett* (London, Gollancz, 1964)

Robert Giddings: *The Tradition of Smollett* (London, Methuen) 1967
Robert Giddings: 'Smollett and the West Indian Connexion' in Robert
Giddings: *The Author, The Book & The Reader* (London, Greenwich
Exchange) 1991
M.A.Goldberg: *Smollett and the Scottish School* (University of New
Mexico Pres, Albuqurque, New Mexico) 1959
Damian Grant: *Tobias Smollett: A Study in Style* (Manchester,
Manchester University Press) 1977
Lionel Kelly: *Tobias Smollettt: The Critical Heritage* (London,
Routledge, 1987)
G.S.Rousseau: *Tobias Smollett: Essays of Two Decades* (Edinburgh, T
& T Clark, 1982)
Rousseau, G.S., and Bouce, P.G. (editors) *Tobias Smollett,
Bicentennial Essays* Presented to L.M.Knapp (New York, Oxford
University Press 1971)
Robert Donald Spector: *Tobias George Smollett* (New York, Twayne,
1968)

(d) Literary and Historical Background
Jeremy Black, editor: *Britain in the Age of Walpole* (London,
Macmillan 1987)
John Butt and Geoffrey Carnall: *The Age of Johnson* 1740-1789
(Oxford, Clarendon Press 1979)
James L. Clifford editor: *Eighteenth Century Literature* (New York,
Oxford University Press 1959)
A.S.Collins: *Authorship in the Days of Johnson* (1927)
David Daiches: *The Paradox of Scottish Culture: The Eighteenth
Century Experience* (London, 1964)
M.D.George: *London Life in the 18th Century* (London, Longman
1925)
M.A.Goldberg: *Smollett and the Scottish School: Studies in 18th
Century Thought* (Albquerque, New Mexico, 1959)
Paul Langford:*A Polite and Commercial People: England 1727-1783*
(Oxford, Oxford University Press, 1989)
Dorothy Marshall: *Eighteen Century England* (London, Longman
1962)
Peter Mathias: *The First Industrial Nation: An Economic History of
Britain 1700-1914* (London, Methuen 1969)
Robert Mayo: *The English Novel in Magazines 1740-1815* (London,
1962)

A.A.Parker: *Literature and the Delinquent: The Picaresque Novel in Spain and Europe 1599-1753* (Edinburgh, 1967)

Ronald Paulson: *Satire and the Novel in 18th Century England* (Yale University Press 1967)

Roy Porter: *English Society in the 18th Century* (Harmondsworth, Penguin 1982)

John Prebble: *Culloden* (Harmondsworth, Penguine 1966)

John Sekora: *Luxury: The Concept in Western Thought, Eden to Smollett* (Baltimore, Maryland, Johns Hopkins University Press 1972)

T.C.Smout: *A History of the Scottish People 1560-1830* (Collins, 1969)

W.A.Speck: *Society and Literature in England 1700-1760* (Dublin, 1983)

A.S.Turbeville (editor) *Johnson's England: An Account of the Life and Manners of His Age* (2 volumes, Oxford, Oxford University Press 1933)

Basil Williams: *The Whig Supremacy 1714-63* (Oxford, Clarendon Press, second edition 1985).